Teaching Literature
in High School

Teaching Literature in High School

Principles into Purposeful Practice

Thomas M. McCann and John V. Knapp

ROWMAN & LITTLEFIELD
Lanham • Boulder • New York • London

Published by Rowman & Littlefield
An imprint of The Rowman & Littlefield Publishing Group, Inc.
4501 Forbes Boulevard, Suite 200, Lanham, Maryland 20706
www.rowman.com

86-90 Paul Street, London EC2A 4NE, United Kingdom

Copyright © 2022 by Thomas M. McCann and John V. Knapp

R. Kikuo Johnson's drawing "Tech Support," October 23, 2017, *The New Yorker*, is reprinted by permission of R. Kikuo Johnson.

All rights reserved. No part of this book may be reproduced in any form or by any electronic or mechanical means, including information storage and retrieval systems, without written permission from the publisher, except by a reviewer who may quote passages in a review.

British Library Cataloguing in Publication Information Available

Library of Congress Cataloging-in-Publication Data Available

ISBN 9781475860245 (cloth) | ISBN 9781475860252 (pbk.) | ISBN 9781475860269 (electronic)

Contents

Preface vii

Acknowledgments xi

Introduction xiii

1 Making Reading Literature Worthwhile 1
2 Options for Frontloading Encounters with Complex Texts 11
3 What We Notice and How We Construct Meaning 29
4 As Patterns Emerge: Joining along and Questioning Why 43
5 Introducing Competing Critical Views 59
6 Responding to Literature in Discussion and Writing 75
7 Experiencing Literature as Performance 91
8 Fostering a Reading Habit 109
9 Connecting Texts in Coherent Inquiry Units 117

Appendix: "Poor Alfred, Buried Three Times" 133

References 137

Index 143

About the Authors 149

Preface

In our earlier book *Learning to Enjoy Literature: How Teachers Can Model and Motivate*, we introduced and demonstrated ways to help students to learn a discipline for reading literary texts. We reasoned that when learners develop a strong facility at reading complex texts and can engage with others in conversations about texts, they come to enjoy their reading experience and feel confident about tackling rich literary texts independently. But we recognize from our long experience in teaching literature from fifth grade through graduate school that students develop their reading facility through much practice over time. So, we offer this follow-up volume containing some nine chapters detailing explicit activities that make for students' purposeful practice: repeating activities that improve one's mastery of the discipline—that of reading imaginative literature with understanding and enjoyment.

While some examples in this volume feature suggestions about relatively simple stories, like the Dr. Seuss tale, *And to Think I Saw It on Mulberry Street* (chapter 5), others illustrate learning how to read more complex stories and plays that high school students typically read or view for class. These include such theatrical classics as Shakespeare's *Julius Caesar* and *Macbeth* (chapter 7), films like Mary McCarthy's *The Group* (1966), short stories like Shirley Jackson's "The Lottery" and Kurt Vonnegut's "Harrison Bergeron" (chapter 5), and unknown authorial tales such as "Poor Alfred, Buried Three Times" (chapter 4).

These more complex works might help answer the question that Ceridwen Dovey asked in a *New Yorker* essay (2015) a few years ago: "Can reading make you happier?" We offer another question: "Can critical practice make you more skilled in reading literature so you could answer Dovey's question?" We answer with an enthusiastic *yes* to both questions; however, we add a caveat: good literature can also make one sad, impatient, angry, and/or even energized to go out and *do* something. At somewhat different times, complex literature may also cause the reader to sit quietly, think deep or ponder over unusual thoughts, and speculate about the seemingly endless choice of paths ahead. However, before consuming literature that can help students experience any of those feelings, they must first learn *how* to read a complex work of literary artistry in order to generate those feelings, not merely ones of incomprehension.

In our earlier *Learning to Enjoy Literature: How Teachers Can Model and Motivate*, we suggested to teachers that mastering the texts mentioned and planning to teach some (or all) of the activities we offer will indeed help students to learn how to make good use of the works they read. In a sense, the earlier book introduces principles for a discipline in reading of literature and offers sample learning activities to immerse students in specific procedures. But developing any degree of mastery of the procedures for careful and critical reading requires a great deal of practice.

Getting swallowed inside a good book or story can be a transformative experience for bewildered teenagers, whose minds and bodies are developing in huge leaps and bounds, but often irregularly, seeming to expand with neither rhyme nor reason to the ones inhabiting such selves. Dovey (2015) argues that during the points common to everyone's life, what she calls "life-juncture transitions"—for example, failing an important test; or winning acceptance into a program, sports team, or college; losing the companionship of a former beloved; or suffering the loss of a parent, sibling, or friend—reading the right play, or narrative, or poem can become crucial. Reading an appropriate story or the experience of watching a play or film may help boost one's spirits, or improve one's ability to empathize with another, or allow one to speculate how a character's thinking helps a sensitive reader/viewer to act with better and more accurate social perceptions (cf. "Social Minds," 2011).

Essentially, borrowing some language from computer programming, a good reader can *Beta Test* real life through the right book or tale, *if understood*, at the right time. As Hamlet once said, "aye, there's the rub." The condition, *if understood*, even only provisionally, might be the key both to the usefulness and to the resulting joy and illumination of experiencing an artistically impressive work of literature. We are happy to recognize that in so many high school literature classes, the democratic virtues of social justice, compassion for others less fortunate than one's self, and greater understanding for those who come from different ethnic worlds, religious practices, and social groups have all come to the forefront in recent years.

We also suspect that text selection and classroom activities for such admirable social values might have eclipsed an equally important and logically prior value: that of learning *how* to read a book with understanding. While selecting literary works for class and then teaching them often cautionary tales of how a character or group rose up to reclaim her/his or their right to a more humane social world (and rightfully so), what might be neglected is teaching the skills and discipline that novice readers need to do what their instructors have already accomplished: how to read complex artworks with sensitivity and skill, works promoting or arguing for values that few reasonable people could argue against. Before one can comprehend masterpieces of literary works to advocate for greater humane values through literature and/or great films, the novice must first learn the reading and/or viewing skills associated with what they have witnessed. The learning of procedures for reading and evaluating comes only with extended practice.

We offer this book as a resource for students' reading and reflecting on complex texts, and then practicing the several procedures that mature readers have learned to apply during reading. In a sense, this is a practice book and a complement to our earlier *Learning to Enjoy Literature: How Teachers can Model and Motivate*. It is not enough to have only a few experiences in reading texts closely, engaging with others in applying a variety of critical views, joining peers in extensive conversations, and writing elaborated responses about literature. As experienced teachers know, learners need practice, practice, practice. We hope that this book offers practices that will engage and motivate your learners.

Acknowledgments

We are indebted to the work of Peter Rabinowitz, James Phelan, Michael W. Smith, and Jeffrey D. Wilhelm for their influences on our thinking about narratives and how we can teach students how to read narratives closely and critically.

We are grateful to Reid Kikuo Johnson for allowing us to reprint his drawing "Tech Support." We also thank the family of Nora O'Flynn for allowing us to retell Nora's story of "Poor Alfred, Buried Three Times."

We appreciate the thoughtful contributions of early career teachers Jaemee Cordero, Amanda De La O, Keaton Fahnestock, Jeff Jakubik, Jessica Morris, and Samantha Panek. We are also grateful to our many high school and university students over decades for their willingness to join enthusiastically into many inquiries into significant literary texts. We also thank several students who allowed us to reproduce their postings to online discussions: Haylie Berkland, Allison Jasinski, Amori Love, Autumn South, Danielle Tinkoff, Katie Torres, and Matthew Wolkober.

The examples of instructional activities in this book come from lessons we have taught and we have shared with colleagues. We appreciate the insightful critical comments from Elizabeth Kahn, Carolyn C. Walter, Beth McFarland-Wilson, Shannon McMullen, and Gabrielle Caputo. We have also gained much from the insights of master teachers Joseph Flanagan, Dawn Forde, and Andy Bouque. We are grateful to Mike Segal of Harriton High School, Rosemont, Pennsylvania, for sharing instructional material.

John expresses his gratitude for Tom's deep understanding of how students and faculty in contemporary public schools work and learn. He also thanks Tom for all his hard work and imagination in pulling together the manuscript for this book and his diligence in improving John's parts of the whole. He is grateful for the support of his many friends and colleagues at Northern

Illinois University's English Department, and his many fellow editors and his friends at NIU's journal, *Style*. He also wants to thank all of his own teachers whose skills and concerns have, over the years, helped shape his own teaching and scholarship.

John also wants to mention his love to all members of his family: his late parents, Victor and Anne Knapp; his two sisters, Shirley Ann Carroll and her adult children and Sean Carroll; Michelle Lugg; and his late sister, Janet Marie Discenza and her adult son, Jeremy. In particular, John sends his love to his four daughters Margaret Anne Knapp; Lara Maria Cantuti, husband Eric, and grandson, Steph'ane; Joanna Haskin, and grandson, Jack Saltzberg; Jennifer Joy Schmeiser, husband Brian, and granddaughters Abi Joy Schmeiser, and Emily Joy Schmeiser. Finally, John expresses his deep appreciation and affection for his wife, Joan Schwarz, whose love and support over the years has helped make him a better man.

Tom continues to be grateful to John Knapp, his first university literature teacher and his methods teacher. Tom is indebted to John in many ways, especially for his willingness to collaborate on three books. Tom thanks his colleagues and students at Northern Illinois University, especially those who contribute to the English education program: Elizabeth A. Kahn, Judy Pokorny, Beth McFarland-Wilson, Carolyn C. Walter, Jeff Levin, and Mary Kay Albamonte. Tom cherishes the steady support of his wife Pamela Gentile McCann, his daughter Katherine Carlson, and his son-in-law Alex Carlson.

We also thank editor Dr. Tom Koerner from Rowman & Littlefield Publishers. We are grateful for his appreciation of the merits of the project and for his attentive work in advancing the book from initial conception to finished product. We appreciate also the contributions of editor Carlie Wall and the many hands of the editorial and production staffs at Rowman & Littlefield for their careful attention to this work.

Introduction

If you visit middle school or high school English classrooms across the United States, you are likely to see that a few enduring approaches to teaching literature remain dominant. It is common to see teachers assign students texts to read, sometimes by portioning out sections of novels or plays. On the day when the reading has been designated for completion, you often see teachers administering quizzes. The practice of quizzing learners might be a teacher's well-intended means for assessing students' proficiencies at comprehending texts. Often, the quizzes serve as a threat to "motivate" students to read.

It is hard to imagine that the practice of assigning and assessing will teach students *how* to read complex literary texts and inspire an enthusiasm for reading literature. Teachers might report that they have enjoyed great success with the assign-and-assess routine, and we can appreciate such reports if "success" means that students comply with the teacher's commands and that many of the learners pass the quizzes. But many teachers of literature seek alternatives to these routines, especially if they embrace a responsibility to explicitly *teach* the procedures for reading complex texts and to cultivate an enthusiasm for reading over time.

WHAT IS "READING CLOSELY"?

How have the skills of "close reading" been labeled? A look into English classrooms over the last fifty years reveals a relatively small number of literary theories and/or techniques taught in the schools, albeit with some small adjustments in vocabulary and emphasis. The first of these stances has been labeled since the 1940s as the New Criticism. While familiar enough in this new century to have become fairly invisible as a specific literary theory, New

Criticism has been for years taken on iconic status and so has been referred to merely as "close readings of the text."

THE NEW CRITICISM, TEXTUAL ANALYSIS, AND STUDENTS' ASSESSMENTS

In searching for alternatives to the dominant yet unsatisfying classroom routines for teaching literature, a teacher might ask, "How did New Criticism come to dominate in schools?" Typically, in many teacher education programs in English, master teachers now expect of their charges trained in the (old) New Criticism to teach via organized, even brilliant, but hopefully brief, lectures. In later years, these were often partly dismissed as acting like a sage-on-the-stage. Consequently, novice teachers are told to pay close attention to the words and sentences of the text and to ask their students to regularly practice in-class writing bursts about the texts. In addition, students were required occasionally to employ small group work, and even to encourage novice student "performances," or one-person lecture-like reports. These have remained the pattern for teaching for several decades (cf. Knapp, 2008, pp. 31–37).

For example, in the cousin-discipline of history, Samual Wineburg (2018) described, analogously, a typical classroom as teachers introducing each topic by using a textbook or giving short lectures. "To make sure students shared a common framework, teachers designed each lesson around the much-maligned I-R-E (Initiation-Response-Evaluation) format: first the teacher would pose a question, a student would respond, and then teachers would nod approval or offer a correction. Students then reassembled in small groups, analyzing original sources [in literary terms, the text] and reconvene for a class discussion."

In English classrooms, teachers intentionally follow a similar lesson format to make "the act of struggling with different interpretations a predictable routine, a way to instill and solidify habits of mind: habits demanding repetition, stick-to-itiveness, and exposure to multiple examples where the content changes but the core intellectual moves remain constant." The common routine suggests that the teacher regularly ask: "What's the first thing we do when we look at a document?" In the history classroom, students would be expected to respond in unison: "Source!" (pp. 127–128). In a literature classroom, an appropriate response would be: "Whose character's voice?"

Sam Wineburg and colleagues were ecstatic about how well this sort of teaching and this particular class worked, creating "materials that put historical thinking at the center," until it came time for assessment. Unfortunately, this was where "history testing showed a poverty of assessment": multiple-choice items "ripping facts from context," confirming students' belief that "what matters most in history [was] a good memory," or College Boards' document-based questions (DBQs), requiring up to a dozen sources, a thesis, and proofreading, all [done] within a single hour (p. 131).

In university classes, such close-reading habits of mind became similarly developed. Unfortunately, the resulting assessments often required students' prodigious feats of memory; novice readers were asked questions about what they called "impossible-to-study-for" evaluations: "Name the one irreducibly artistic quality found in Book Nine of Milton's *Paradise Lost*?" Or, "In Saul Bellow's *Henderson, the Rain King*, how did Henderson's trip to Africa parallel or oppose Odysseus's visit to Ithaca after his twenty-year absence?" Or, "What is wrong with the question a critic asked: 'How many children had Lady Macbeth?'"

In brief, one of the major assessment problems with evaluations inside the New Criticism teaching model was the gaping contrast between students as first-time readers vs. their professors' *rereading* experiences. It was in the very nature of life experience that older consumers (teachers) of literature who were "reading against memory," to use Peter Rabinowitz's terms, often expected almost impossible retrieval skills by those ten to thirty years younger, during (usually) first-time single readings (*Authorizing*, pp. 90–102).

Add to this very large and different sets of experiences between the two age cohorts with any given novel, play, or lyric poem. As mentioned above, the standard pedagogy during the height of the New Critical wave of scholarship was the lecture. Many teachers were taught to be sages-on-the-stage, with each teacher typically teaching several sections in a given school day, days where students were supposed to fill notebooks and still had to exercise prodigious memories. These became the hallmarks of the good students. Reasoned-out, analytic literary problems to solve were thus more often displays of the teacher rather than as student-comprehension exemplars.

In brief, just as in certain history class's assessments, memory was king—instead of reasoning and feeling. When it came to posing questions for first-time literary readers (and specifying the answers), many literature teachers forgot that they were relying on their own decades-long development and knowledge from multiple readings for identifying and labeling textual specifics. From these limitations, and despite other shifts in the culture outside the schools and colleges, popular methods of teaching New Criticism, as well as favored techniques of sharing literature experiences in classrooms, had barely evolved during the 1940s through the mid-1960s (Cuban, 1999).

Nevertheless, the assumptions that teachers stood tall like orchestra leaders, waving a textual baton at their 30+ band members dwindled by the late 1960s and early 1970s, and New Criticism started to move into cliché territory, soon losing its singular allure, especially at the secondary level. Similar to changing urban neighborhoods retaining their original but aging individuals, so too did many veteran teacher's New Critical behavioral patterns solidify selected methods that appeared to achieve results in a variety of the humanities, particularly in textual studies in literature, languages, and history (cf. Wellek & Warren, 1949). Nonetheless, New Criticism and many of its once beyond-obvious teaching techniques eventually gave way to refocused reader-response (RR) methods of teaching.

READER-RESPONSE CRITICISM AND RELATED TEACHING

A book that greatly helped cause New Criticism's replacement, albeit mostly ignored for its first thirty years, was Louise Rosenblatt's *Literature as Exploration* (1976/1938). Once her original ideas were disinterred in the mid-1970s, she brought out, some two years later, her *The Reader, the Text, the Poem (1978),* and her pedagogical concepts suddenly received the recognition in high school classrooms that had been eluding it for three decades. Rosenblatt helped generate the teaching technique called, ultimately, Reader Response (RR) criticism

Rather than placing the majority of his/her attention to the pages between a book's covers, teachers practicing RR practices moved students' attention from the text, and diminishing the teacher's expertise about it, back to the audience—the reader. Sad to say, in the new masterplan of teaching, the instructor and his/her literary expertise shrank in importance, and the teacher's value was attributed to acting more as a "guide-on-the-side." Lo and behold, teachers discovered, using RR techniques, that novice readers had a LOT to say about the book. Inevitably, since the leader's expertise mattered less than the individuals' opinions, of which, in a thirty-member classroom, differing opinions typically numbered between twenty-five and thirty.

The practical effect in the RR-dominated classroom has indeed increased student conversation and in-class argumentation, but often came at the cost of reduced reasoned disputation. This in spite of Rosenblatt's warnings of what happens when primary attention was paid to memorial reconstruction and individual affect (Knapp, p. 39). Many teachers came to rely on a single over-arching methodology in the classroom: entering into conversations initiated by learners' personal responses to texts.

Michael W. Smith (Rabinowitz & Smith, 1998) said twenty years later that "emphasis on the pedagogy of personal experience runs the risk of homogenizing what students get to read and mitigates against experiencing the uncomfortable growth that can occur when they have to face a character whose life is much different from their own" (p. 134). Just as cultural lag kept the New Criticism (or variations thereof) in play to this day, so too does RR find some teachers confusing students' reciting relatively unsubstantiated personal preferences with developing abilities of literary analysis. In another context, the rhetorician Stanley Fish (1980) has wisely pointed out that "while, in some classrooms, teachers disavow interpretation in favor of merely presenting the text; but it is actually a gesture in which one set of interpretive principles is replaced by another that . . . claims for itself the virtue of not being an interpretation at all" (p. 45).

A NEW SYNTHESIS, A RETURN OF THE REPRESSED, OR A VENTURE INTO NEW TERRITORY?

In the third decade of the new century, some blend, or a mix-and-match gumbo of the two persistent critical practices, New Criticism and RR, prevailed. Of course, both also exhibit certain strengths: New Criticism asks students to read closely and interpret the language nuances in prose fiction, while RR suggested that students observe their own pulses as they read or observe characters' behaviors and the choices they make.

For teachers who are long-time advocates of "pedagogical content knowledge," the synthesis *of* a new literature pedagogy should become quite familiar: content knowledge, pedagogical techniques, and supportive classroom environments (McCann & Knapp, 2019, pp. 146–147). And, along with the clear advantages for having learned at least some of the elements of the two models, literature teachers and students can move toward recognizing that comprehending a work of literary art is "both a solitary act and a social engagement, activities that interpenetrate one another in dynamic and often unpredictable ways" (McCann & Knapp, 2019, p. 41).

One of the major movements in literary scholarship has been called *distributed cognition* or, more colloquially, *social minds* (cf. Palmer, 2011). Among those arguing for teaching techniques that move away from the more formulaic applications of New Criticism and RR, but still building upon some of its more useful elements, is Alan Palmer in his *Social Minds*. He suggests that "systems of socially distributed cognition may have interesting cognitive properties of their own . . . group properties that differ considerably from the properties of individuals" (Palmer, 2004, p. 164).

Palmer argues that for literary study, we should bring the social qualities in learning about literature to the forefront and, at times, consider solitary analyses as secondary. This book, in tandem with related works (McCann, 2014; McCann & Knapp, 2019; McCann & Knapp, 2021), suggests some classroom activities that will offer ways of illuminating literary and dramatic works like those under consideration but also help students look a little closer at their own emotions via their classmates' responses and reactions to them as they read.

As individuals consume a text or film, what language or scene triggers a given viewer/reader, and how does one expand his/her emotional and cognitive awareness through discussions (not recitations) with classmates, friends, and colleagues? What are the features that distinguish discussions in action and the rudiments of initiating and managing peer conversations about reading and thinking about great works of literary, film, and dramatic art?

WHAT THIS BOOK OFFERS

As you make your way through this book, it might remind you of the earlier *Learning to Enjoy Literature* (McCann & Knapp, 2021). That's no coincidence. This book is intended as an extension of the earlier text and offers additional models and possibilities for practice. The classroom practices sponsored in this book break with the dominant assign-and-assess model of teaching literature. The book offers ways for teachers to *demonstrate procedures* for reading complex literary texts and options that invite students to *practice the procedures*.

There are times when the nature of the text and the needs of the learners require some preparation for the reading experience. Chapter 2 offers options for "frontloading" encounters with complex texts, with examples of pre-reading activities that are likely to help students to tap prior knowledge, build background knowledge, and think critically about characters and themes from a work of literature. Chapter 3 offers some evocative visual images for analysis and then advances toward practicing the same intellectual moves with simple texts. In doing so, teachers can help novice literary learners how to discover the "Rules of Notice" and the "Rules of Signification."

Chapter 4 offers ways of helping learners to construct meaning from complex texts. Often, teachers ask students to provide text-based responses to questions, and students happily comply by quoting passages. But how does a reader know what to quote and how to explain to others how the elements in the text convey some meaning? As this chapter demonstrates, attention to various patterns and building toward an overall configuration, learners can anticipate narrative structures, recognize ruptures to such structures, and question the implications of structures and ruptures.

Chapter 5 invites readers to consider texts through several critical lenses. Without getting too technical and esoteric, teachers can foster in students an awareness of several critical views of a text that can prompt learners to reexamine their reading and discover where their voice can contribute to the conversation about various ways to understand and evaluate a work of literature. The chapter argues that an awareness of the competing ways for reading a text is necessary for framing the problems that give significance to written responses about a work.

Chapter 6 acknowledges that readers deepen their understanding when they talk extensively about texts and write about texts. The chapter offers general principles for helping teachers to facilitate genuine discussions about literature and suggests ways to prepare learners for their written responses to their reading.

Chapters 7 and 8 extend the work on teaching the procedures for reading literary texts by suggesting how to prepare learners to perform scenes from literature and reflect on the implications of the performances and by suggesting how to structure independent reading efforts to vary and encourage the habit of reading literature. Chapter 7 demonstrates that students' viewing and enacting performances of selected scenes from a drama or a narrative episode can provide learners with insights that apply to the work as whole.

The book includes a chapter titled "Fostering a Reading Habit." The teacher of literature wants more than shepherding students through a sequence of complex texts. Instruction in the study of literature should inspire a pleasurable habit of reading a variety of literary texts and not discourage readers' independent exploration.

Finally, chapter 9 argues that although previous chapters focus on the work with individual texts, strategic teachers consider the connections among texts as students inquire into compelling concepts and resonant themes. Teachers might think first about how to engage learners in lines of inquiry that students find consequential and then select texts that support the inquiry. This perhaps reverses the typical process for selecting works of literature that serve as the backbone for an English language arts curriculum, providing a coherent framework for connecting works that in a sense "speak to each other" and take on greater significance in an inquiry context than they would considering when in isolation.

Chapter 1

Making Reading Literature Worthwhile

Teachers of literature face a daunting task. While the teacher might delight in the pleasures of reading imaginative tales and experiencing engrossing dramas, many students do not share such passion, largely because the struggle with complex works of literature does not seem worth the effort. Many years before the idea of flipped classrooms became a buzzword for several secondary English teachers, a new teacher might find her first teaching job in a small rural high school filled with the children of dairy and wheat farmers. These are students who work for two to three hours before class and, unless (sometimes, even though) they participate in sports, music, or other afternoon activities, and in some instances toil for some hours after school as well.

Another new teacher might find herself in a large city public school with 3,000 students, representing multiple languages from multiple countries. Some of these learners are quite proficient in social uses of English, while others are barely conversant in English, and some may even be functionally illiterate in their language of origin. These students have a difficult time learning both the skills associated with literacy in any language and, simultaneously, literacy in contemporary English. Hence, in recent decades, teaching literature successfully has never been more difficult.

In addition, the sirens' songs of TV, films, smartphones, and social media have made technological distractions even more likely that students have little time, extra or otherwise, to read complete novels or Shakespearian plays in or outside of school. Couple those student limitations with the multidimensional tasks of teachers whose courses demand fulfilling literature and writing requirements, and there is no need explaining to thousands of English teachers how difficult their professional world has become.

Not only are most of their students exhibiting difficulties in basic literary reading and expositional writing skills, but they are also taught by teachers who may be among the hardest working of any in the school curriculum with loads of 100 or more student papers to evaluate per week. Inevitably, any attention a teacher gives to detailed analyses of literary works at the expense of teaching writing develops instructional guilt complexes that are rarely mollified if or when the balance swings the other way.

There seems never to be enough class time to do a decent job with both the literary work and the writings about it. Unfortunately, when those classes focus on the nuts and bolts of student writing expression alone, they often seem to lack something, some spice, while straining to invent and develop interesting writing topics. On the other hand, for some faculty, teaching literature alone is often considered a self-indulgence by those whose primary concern is developing the synthetic interactions between reading and writing.

Teachers may already know the history of their discipline and its needed metacognitive steps (or thinking about how to do mental work inside the disciplines of teaching literature or writing), but the problems are almost always centered around time available or balancing competing needs (Holt-Reynolds, 1999). So, given the built-in constraints on instructors, how can we help students, especially those reluctant readers, to *enjoy* what they're required to read or encourage to read?

Before the learners can "enjoy" their reading, teachers will need to develop some strategies to encourage nonreaders or reluctant readers just to open the book and begin the process (cf. Wilhelm & Smith, 2014, pp. 32–45). At the same time, how do we help the poor overworked teachers spend their time more usefully interacting with their students—loaded more toward mutual and pleasurable engagement in the stories in class. Obviously enough, such interactions about both reading and writing about those readings are crucial for student success (Reisman, 2015).

"FREE" READING AND THE DISCIPLINE OF READING LITERATURE

Some scholars of pedagogy advocate "fixing" the problem of teaching adolescents to read literature critically by letting their charges read whatever they wish, what is called "free voluntary reading," advocated by the author Stephen Krashen, in a book with that very title (2011). While parents are pleased if their children do enjoy school, they all too often also insist that, in the language and literature classrooms, their growing progeny learn some basic literary and reading skills.

What are poor teachers to do with so many tugs on their time and energy? And what's a poor student to do if the learner is a struggling or an indifferent reader, one who just never became skilled enough in the lower grades to enjoy the pleasures of the text in the upper grades? (Wineberg, 2016). One who never felt the emotional and intellectual satisfactions that committed readers of particular genres experience, even those focusing only on the popular genres of romance, vampire stories, horror, dystopian fiction, and fantasy.

As reported in their useful book, Wilhelm and Smith (2014) completed an "in-depth exploration of the nature and variety of the pleasures avid adolescent readers take in their out-of-school reading" (p. 9). They observe that the popular texts adolescents read on their own "are often marginalized or dismissed by teachers and other adults." Wilhelm and Smith argue that "by sharing some ideas for how we can *make reading for pleasure* more central to the work we do in and out of schools to promote reading and literacy, and by exploring what benefits might accrue if we do so" might be the way to fly (emphasis added, p. 9). Elsewhere, Janice A. Radway (1986) has argued that we have "failed to detect the essential complexity" [characterizing] "the interaction between people and mass-produced culture" (p. 10; see more recently, Carr, 2010).

As helpful as Wilhelm and Smith's arguments about literary pleasures are, the pedagogical practices suggested in this book address some of the significant problems faced by contemporary teachers and students in literature classes. Reading is profoundly social, requiring readers engaging not only with the teachers in the room, as well as fellow age-mates, but also including detailed interactions with the author and narrators (Knapp, 2008, p. 94). Unfortunately, no matter the efforts of some of the best traditional teachers, many kids come home groaning about the boring required stuff written long before they were even born, and what's the fun in that? They especially don't even like the fact that the teacher is usually the only one talking, even though the teacher sometimes seems to invite conversation by asking questions nobody has much to say about. As one scholar points out, in many classrooms, "typically just one person . . . learns from engaging with and responding to [all of] an assigned work of literature . . . the teacher!" (Weismann, p. 2). Most students, on the other hand, only engage with a single other reader: that same teacher.

Wouldn't it be useful if everyone in class also interacted with everyone else concerning each one's writing about the commonly read literary work (Knapp, 2008, p. 37; Weissman, 2016)? Ironically, teacher-educators acknowledge in a study done in the late 1980s and 1990s that in many, if not most, English classrooms, the academic conversations either initiated by or primarily among students comprise about 2 percent to 3 percent of all classroom talk (Nystrand et al., 1997).

In mutually active exploration, most students begin reading a complex work of literature by saying, if only to themselves: "'I feel . . . I don't know what I feel.' From this helpless and oppressed condition, [he/she] extricated [him/herself] by doing something. . . . That something . . . is to make a language—not as a simple naming but [one that] becomes exploratory once it ceased to be automatic" (Davis, p. 12). It's clear that the strongest motivators to help reluctant readers to begin or to continue their reading are (1) an enthusiastic, well-informed teacher; (2) one or more peers whose excitement about a given text energizes a fellow learner; (3) an artist work (novel, play, poetry, film) that captures something the readers already thinks is, or can be persuaded to feel, important. At the heart of such a system are concerns Barbara Rogoff (1990) asked some thirty years ago: Do we teachers as adults "adjust activities to children or are children responsible for adjusting to the adult world?" (p. 21).

Some teachers and scholars have suggested that the best way to engage students as readers is to let them read freely. Support for student-centered choices has not been new over the years in the schools. We have already mentioned Krashen's book and his ideas about voluntary free reading, and the afore-mentioned book titled *Reading Unbound* (2014) by Jeffrey D. Wilhelm and Michael W. Smith, two veteran scholars of literary education theory and practice.

Their basic arguments, as self-confessed "deep and fulfilling" readers of books they loved, have to do with what Jeff suggested was the motivations individuals have by "reading of [their] own free will anticipating the satisfaction [they would get] from the act of reading" as well as continuing "reading because [they were] interested in it," albeit "begun at some else's request" (Wilhelm & Smith, 2014, p. 19). They recognized in their own scholarship that the pleasures of reading were "not front and center" in their minds (2014, p. 17), nor was pleasure paid too much attention to in other reading studies (p. 21). Hence, they "undertook this study" because they wanted to find out "more about how these notions of pleasure in reading played out with adolescents" (p. 26).

LEARNING TO READ LITERATURE AND LEARNING FROM READING LITERATURE

Teachers of literature are likely to agree that a goal is for students to enjoy their reading of literature, but some also see that relatively easily absorbed pleasurable reading is not enough. Wilhelm and Smith (2014), echoing the philosopher John Dewey, point out how "social interest motivates reading," and one obvious social connection "was through [readers'] relationship with characters" (87). Both experienced and preservice teachers should be committed to trying to move their students or themselves deeper into the idea of pleasure from reading further into character by considering what attracted kids to books. Pushing anyone into *pleasure* is regrettable, but there are some alternatives.

In Blakey Vermeule's *Why Do We Care about Literary Characters* (2010), she asks the ultimate question: "What exactly starts the reader off on a stimulating train? Is it the stuff inside the story or is it some aspect of the narrative itself? The content or the form? These are ancient and enduring literary theoretical questions" (p. 45). She goes on to cite two thinkers, Gregory Currie (1997) and Alvin Goldman (2006), the former positing that "[when] we read fiction, we adapt the point of view of a hypothetical 'reader of fact' or 'observer of fact' . . . [because] "a fictional [novel or film] as it opens is an account of events as if they were happening or did happen" (p. 43). "It's difficult to follow a narrative at all without this sort of baseline perspective to all that follows in the work" (Goldman, 2006, p. 287). That "reader of fact learns all about the events in the story." The reader "empathizes with the characters and, insofar as we empathize with him [or her] we do too" (Currie, 1997, pp. 69–71).

Vermeule argues about how "one of the most powerful human imaginative capacities [is] the power and lure of fantasy" (p. 17). She is convinced that the meaningful distinction between fictional and nonfictional characters is not ontological but technological. "Our social brains are just as capable of being stimulated by fiction as our sexual selves are . . . by pornography. In fact, we run our massive inference systems in a decoupled mode all the time: [whenever, for example] we consider what we would do in hypothetical situations" (p. 17).

Another scholar, Angus Fletcher, in *Wonderworks* (2021), considers several of what he calls the "25 most powerful technological inventions in the history of literature" (title). He then connects them to advances in how the mind works when we read stories and tales. Fletcher suggests, for example, that Bible mysteries read aloud to congregations during the "wanning days of the Roman Empire left readers with no particular answer [a]lthough the Bible's faith-stirring enigmas inspired a new literary genre, the mystery plays" (p. 195). Those mysteries and puzzles were labeled insoluble (how could Jesus make wine out of water, or rise from the dead?). These eventually led to tales where certain mysteries *were* solved, and solutions were discovered by professionals we now call "trained detectives."

They used an old logic of *"deduction,* which employed general knowledge to draw conclusions about individual cases" (Fletcher, p. 197). This logic of deduction was "drilled into Medieval Europeans students from the 11th Century University of Bologna to the 17th Century University of Turku" (Estonia) through their memorizing Aristotles's *Metaphysics* or The Bible, moving from generalizations to specific proofs (p. 197). Eventually, thinkers like Sir Francis Bacon grew dissatisfied with Aristotelian-type answers explaining the heliocentric view of the universe.

Instead, Bacon argued that the sun remained (relatively) stable but the earth moved around it, not the reverse. This "new logic was called *induction*—moving from particular facts to general laws—but then using experiments to prove or disprove its conclusion" (197). Of course, one of the problems of inductions was searching from hundreds of specific examples to "prove" a given generalization, and few had the time or energy to do that for all the problems in the world.

Nonetheless, someone named William Whewell coined the term *scientist* to name persons doing this process of moving from induction to deduction to experiment. "Scientists" were actually "sleuths" solving mysteries, and concluded that "the most effective way" to teach "the globe's curious minds" wasn't with textbooks "but with fiction" (p. 201). Fletcher suggests that our "brain learns by making predictions that fail, prompting our neurons to hastily gain more intel and make another prediction" (p. 204).

However, some might have "tried to twist the facts into agreement with [a potentially] flawed hypothesis . . . a neural foible known as confirmation bias . . . manipulating data to support [their] original guess" (p. 205). Fiction writer Edger Allan Poe became fascinated with the step-by-step process of inductive observations, deductive predictions, and the related experiments to prove/disprove the scientist's conclusions.

Poe then wrote "The Murders in the Rue Morgue," which begins with "some random . . . observations about the games of checkers and chess" and "thereby employing an arbitrary narrative of the preface as a secret training device, designed to guide our brain into thinking more scientifically" (pp. 203–204). In developing the process of "predict-then-test method in mystery stories, Poe . . . has uncovered a general rule of our mental behavior" (p. 208), so to explain here the final mystery of "The Murders of the Rue Morgue."

Fletcher asserts, "You'll need to tackle that mystery yourself, spinning predictions from the facts you'll uncover—and then re-spinning your predictions when they propel you into error" (p. 208). Thus, during the nineteenth century, scientists and literary thinkers interacted in ways that could draw in both—those more concerned with hard facts and those literary aficionados—into using one another in solving selected problems that appeared at first to exist on different worlds. In brief, one way of getting novice readers to dig into a literary text, and then, ideally, getting lost in that text, is by presenting the reader with a problem to solve. Thus, reading literature involves inquiry and taps into humans' natural inclinations toward problem-solving and interacting with peers. The teachers' own powers of imagination must be thereby exercised in creating or even borrowing from past history, looking at both Bacon and Poe, for example, to discover the creation of the virtual scientist.

SEEING PATTERNS AND STRUCTURES AND MAKING COMPLEX INFERENCES

The ideas proposed in this book may not be a panacea for the overworked teachers of literature, but they do offer alternatives, Homerically speaking, to the Skylla of too many tasks to attend and the Khraybdis of too little time to complete even the majority of them well. Learning how to reason through storytelling problems and mysteries has, for centuries, been part of the human condition (Homer, 1961; 1998). For different yet excellent examples of such reasoning through, but directed and led by, a teacher, see Helanine Smith (2015).

In addition, the ideas offered in the following chapters at least offer some suggestions that will help both students and teachers enjoy classes where each participates, where discussions move with due deliberation, allowing time to think through reading and offering companionship among people engaged in mutual exploration. This book, as with the earlier *Learning to Enjoy Literature* (McCann & Knapp, 2021), shares ways to help students learn procedures for problem-solving that is specific to the reading of complex works of literature. That book emphasizes two features of teaching and learning: (1) that students learn the procedures for disciplined reading of complex texts through extensive interactions with each other, and (2) that shared inquiry into problems drives the conversations and related reflections on process.

When classrooms do feature multiple cross-transactions with a literary text, all students in the room—and the teacher—discover not only changes in the individual's reading, but that, in some way, the collective sense of that very text is enlarged by each reader's interactions with their peers. For both concepts—learning the procedures for reading and engaging collaboratively in problem-solving—what is needed is relatively simple and yet so difficult to attain in everyday practice. Students will need much practice in order to become aware of procedures that they can readily employ.

Shared inquiry and purposeful peer interactions do tend to take on a life of their own, as students find it enjoyable to learn from one another, and the teacher becomes, mysteriously, less frantic, less directive, yet more impactful. Not every teacher will find the proposed practices of this book easy and attractive, but we urge continued experimentation and exploration into instruction that moves well beyond the common routines of assigning texts to read and then assessing students' recall of their reading.

For those willing to try the learning activities recommended in this book or adapted variations of them, the "mystery" of enjoying the experience of a work of literature is really no mystery at all. Most students need time alone to read quietly, and also need other people with whom to have conversations about their reading. Sometimes, we forget how influential peers can be in encouraging their classmates to read literature and reflect on the experience and meanings (Reisman, 2015).

Start by creating interesting problems to solve. Aristotle and Francis Bacon both saw what they assumed was the same sun. Yet, neither was, at first, satisfied about why day followed night, but differently in May and December. The core problem of movement and what "moved" and what remained (seemingly) fixed was fundamental yet took the latter over 2,000 years to solve, when such "solutions" had been considered, and solved, in other parts of the world. If only received answers to questions had been fundamentally reconsidered earlier.

In order to set interesting ideas and/or reconsiderations about literature in motion, we need to emphasize some basics about generally accepted learning theories, basics that will seem obvious to some but may not for others. Most teachers know intuitively, if not formally, the differences between what those in the cognitive sciences call "ill-formed tasks" contrasted to "well-formed tasks" (Hattie, 2012, pp. 115–137). Feedback is rather different and more-or-less useful, depending on the types of tasks students are engaged in. Much depends on readers' given level of experience with solving puzzles and/or creating solutions to the difficulties they set for themselves or are set jointly with and by their teachers.

Briefly, well-formed or well-structured tasks, typical in too many classrooms, are those that can be "broken down into a fixed sequence of sub-tasks or steps that consistently lead to the same result" (Rosenshine et al., 1996, p. 182). In playing chess, putting the Queen in X position does checkmate the King when he is in Y position, and that means checkmate every time. The Bishop cannot jump ahead directly vertical to save the King, nor can a Knight move five spaces directly sideways to do the same. The King loses in that way every time. Such fixed patterns cannot be altered, neither by some Chess Czar's edict nor by a grandmaster's imaginative reworking the game's basic rules. However, such a description and practice hardly fits what the average novice reader of imaginative fiction does when he/she reads a new novel or story.

By contrast, then, reading literature in a supportive classroom involves what are spoken of instead as "ill-formed or minimally structured tasks." These cannot be "broken down into a fixed sequence of subtasks or steps that consistently lead to a desired end result" (Rosenshine, p. 182). And because they are not characterized by "fixed sequences of subtasks," one cannot "develop algorithms that students use to complete" such tasks that are set to equally please struggling readers and proficient readers together (p. 182).

In brief, there is no formulaic way of learning how to read an imaginative tale or longer work of fiction, even though readers and critics of literature long ago created what are called genres, loosely patterned expectations readers have come to rely upon. These help readers see selected patterns ahead of time concerning what a given author assumes readers will understand. However, there are clues and patterns to look for and remember as we have demonstrated in our earlier work (McCann & Knapp, 2021).

Since human beings have been telling one another stories since well before Homer and his "classic 3,000-year-old *Odyssey*" (Boyd, 2009, p. 232), the singer of tales (as Homer was called) assumed that his listeners, hearing a story about a stranger in an unexplored land, would find some connection, something familiar, between their own experience and the story world into which they had just entered. Novice readers may not realize at first how familiar some fictional genres are as story patterns about human experiences. Scenes, characters, conflicts may all seem different to the novice reader, but to the experienced ones, they can appear quite familiar nonetheless.

While genres are not "characterized by fixed sequences of subtasks," they do point to typical macro-experiences familiar to people of many cultures, religious beliefs, and historical eras. For many millennia, human beings have learned to cope with a world that often takes them one and a half or two decades to learn; they fall in love, create near-duplicates of their species, explore parts of the planet unfamiliar to their parents as well as themselves, join groups to help them in their explorations, and return to find how briefly exploratory time can be as one grows, learns, experiences, and ages.

Although human beings have created many thousands of tales detailing in fine-grained terms how we feel, think, hope, and dream throughout all of these typical Homo sapiens' adventures, not all of them, indeed few of them, last. As Brian Boyd (2009) has argued, because "art involves external forms, the testing mechanism operates in the minds of other humans, in terms of their interests. If a work of art fails to earn attention, it dies" (p. 121).

Boyd's dictum is a variation of Poe's following a "step-by-step process of inductive observations, deductive predictions," and then writing a tale, whose popularity (or not) proves/disproves the scientist's conclusions (p. 203). "If it (the story) succeeds, it can last even for a millennia" (Boyd, p. 121), like Homer's 3-millennia-old "song" of a man named Odysseus, gone to war for twenty years but who returns to his faithful wife, Penelope, and his (by-now) grown-up son, Telemachos. Versions exist in many languages besides Homeric Greek, in verse tales, prose fictions, and contemporary film treatments like the Coen brothers' production of *Oh Brother, Where Art Thou?* In three thousand years, fascinated millions have read or heard or seen it with pleasure and love. So, students can learn to read, interrogate, and enjoy such narratives, especially when the interrogations and enjoyment involve collaborating and sharing with peers.

Teachers who do more than merely assigning and assessing expose their students to the varieties of how literary discoveries/inventions are found/

created. Teachers who engage learners in shared inquiries that require extensive peer interactions to discover and practice procedures that are specific to reading literary texts will find an appreciative community of learners and perhaps influence lifelong readers of literature.

YOUR VIEW

This chapter suggests that most literature instruction in high school amounts to assigning reading and quizzing students in one way or another about their recall of the text. In contrast, this book offers ways to help students to discover disciplined procedures for reading literary texts and to orchestrate opportunities for practice with those procedures. To what extent is this an accurate picture of current practices in school? If it is accurate, what alternatives have you found? You might want to discuss the following questions with some colleagues:

1. What are your impressions of the common practices in teaching literature in high school and at universities? How have you arrived at your impressions?
2. What value do you see in the study of literature, beyond the pleasure that readers enjoy from the vicarious experience of immersing oneself in the narrative?
3. What are the typical challenges that you see in teaching literature at your school? How can you address these challenges?
4. What adjustments will be necessary to the curriculum and to the classroom practices to make the study of literature more enjoyable and impactful for learners?

Chapter 2

Options for Frontloading Encounters with Complex Texts

Teachers sometimes complain about students' reluctance to read works of literature that represent distant times and remote places (McCann, 1996). As the complaint goes, many adolescents find that the texts that they encounter in middle school or high school do not hold their interests, because the language is too complicated and the settings and situations too removed from the students' lives. These perceived faults would apply to all of the works of Shakespeare and most literature of English and the United States before 1900. That would be dismissing a large and significant body of literature.

The apparent logical response to the complaints is to select somehow only those texts that match in language the current reading proficiencies of the learners and that represent settings, characters, and situations that appear to hold an appeal to the vast majority of the students in the school. The hope of teachers acting in this spirit is to connect students with texts with which they will be comfortable. It is a kind of tailoring process—taking the measure of students' Lexile levels and suiting them up with texts with the matching Lexile levels. The alternative is to *prepare* students for their encounter with complex texts, even if there is not a custom match (Wilhelm, Baker, & Dube, 2001). In fact, from a Vygotskian perspective, the more responsible instructional move is to help students to stretch into new levels of text complexity.

Of course, planning the appropriate kind of preparation for students' encounters with a text depends on the immediate instructional goals and knowledge about a particular group of learners. In some instances, the effort will involve building relevant background knowledge. In other instances, a teacher will want to help students to activate the knowledge they already have.

BUILDING BACKGROUND KNOWLEDGE

One pre-reading effort involves the important process of building background knowledge (O'Reilly, Wang, & Sabatini, 2019; Marzano, 2004; Recht & Leslie, 1988). Too often this effort takes the form of the teacher *presenting* to students some information about the author and about the historical context for the narrative or for the author's writing of the text. There are two reasons to be skeptical about such presentations. First, most students gain little from a teacher's attempts to *transmit* knowledge. While a teacher may doggedly present details about an author's life, students are likely to be cognitively invested in their feelings of hunger or their eagerness to gather soon with friends (Csikszentmihalyi & Larson, 1984).

The second reason for seeing a futility in a teacher presenting background information is that the selected details about the author's life or about the time in which the author lived may bear little relevance for the text the students were about to read. You can imagine a teacher lecturing students about flappers and gangsters and bootleg liquor and jazz and the precarious mental state of Zelda Fitzgerald as preparation for reading *The Great Gatsby*. One has to ask, "How is any of this information critical to reading the novel and thinking about its thematic implications or examining Fitzgerald's language closely?"

Teachers are wise to think strategically about what background information is important as an introduction to a complex work of literature and about the means for building background knowledge. For years, teachers have invited students to engage in "web quests," which are intended to be student-directed research efforts that rely on web-based resources. Typically, a teacher outlines the web quest task and identifies web-based resources. A group collaboration alternative would be a modest research project that asks students to gather selected information as it might apply to the reading of a work of literature.

The following example illustrates the possibility for teams of students to gather information that can support the reading of a novel. The effort requires teamwork, research, writing, and oral presentation. The idea of the brief written reports is that they can be compiled and duplicated or posted online. In a sense, the product of this effort is a kind of Cliff's Notes for the novel that students are about to read, with the shared information providing the background that can inform the reading of a complex text. Unlike Cliff's Notes, the compiled document is the product of the students' effort and does not supplant the reading of the work of literature itself.

GROUP RESEARCH PROJECT

Charles Dickens

A Tale of Two Cities

Supposition: Now that the former president has retired from office and left the White House, he has considerable leisure time on his hands. Since his days as an undergraduate, the former president has had an interest in reading the works of Charles Dickens; but the president's involvement in politics and government has occupied his attention and prevented him from studying the English novelist whom he admires. The former president recognizes that the works of Dickens present some challenges to the modern reader. He knows that by having knowledge about the author and about the historical era that influenced the work, a reader can have greater understanding of a challenging text. With your help in providing relevant background information, the former president hopes to be able to read, understand, and enjoy the novels of Charles Dickens. The former president invites you to prepare brief reports that will help him to enjoy and appreciate the novels of Dickens, especially *A Tale of Two Cities*. Books in the school library and in the public library, as well as electronic reference material, should help you to complete your research. Remember that you are going to study the material, synthesize the information, and summarize it. *Be careful to avoid plagiarism*: you are going to process and summarize what you have found instead of merely copying the writing of others. You might choose to cite short passages and give credit to the source. After you have thoroughly researched the topic, you should produce a written and an oral report. Each group should choose a topic from *each* group of topics. You may have to negotiate your choices with other groups so that we avoid redundancies. Here are the topics:

Group A: Topics related to London, Paris, and the French Revolution (*Choose One*)

1. Louis XVI and Marie Antoinette
2. The Bastille
3. The "Tennis Court Oath" and the National Assembly
4. The Causes for the French Revolution
5. The Reign of Terror
6. War and politics in England in the mid- to late eighteenth century
7. Highwaymen and transportation in England in the late eighteenth century

Group B: Dickens' Life and Work *(Choose One)*

1. Dickens' career as a journalist
2. Dickens' childhood and formal education
3. Dickens' approach to publishing fiction and its effect on his work
4. Dickens' marriage and family life
5. Dickens reputation as a writer and his literary career
6. Evidence of social criticism in Dickens' novels
7. Dickens interest in politics and revolution

Although the former president has a keen mind, he has little tolerance for vague abstraction and excessive verbiage. Your presentations, therefore, must meet specific requirements.

Written Report: Your written report should take the form of a one-page, typed, single-spaced memo directed to the former president. The language should be clear and concise. Specific, concrete examples are preferred to vague, abstract generalizations. This memo should *not exceed one page*, but it should *not be less than one page*. The memo will be duplicated to share with the rest of the class. Be sure, then, that you have carefully proofread and edited so that your work is ready for publication.

Oral Presentation: The oral report should convey the *essence* of your written report. You are encouraged to use visual aids or other support that will help make your presentation concrete and entertaining.

In some instances, a teacher might hesitate with the frontloading of instruction about a particular work of literature for fear of revealing too much or spoiling some of the pleasures of the reading experience. It seems unlikely, however, that students knowing something about the French Revolution or the life and social commentary of Charles Dickens would reveal too much of the plot of *A Tale of Two Cities* or restrict readers' critical assessment or creative reading of the text.

STARTING SIMPLY

Many teachers attempt to prime students for their reading of a complex text by writing in a journal about a prompt that might challenge learners to think empathically about characters or judge thematic possibilities. Prompting such writing and facilitating the subsequent discussion are relatively simple routines that can position students to read a text critically. Here are a few examples of such journal writing prompts:

- When, if ever, might a person be justified in breaking the law? Describe a circumstance when someone thinks that he or she is justified in breaking

a rule or a law. On what grounds would the person justify the behavior? To what extent do you agree with this justification? (possible connections: *Their Eyes Were Watching God, Beloved, Of Mice and Men, Fahrenheit 451,* or *One Flew Over the Cuckoo's Nest*)
- Heroes aren't always mighty warriors. In fact, everyday heroes can be relatively humble people who complete a difficult journey (physical or experiential) or overcome a significant obstacle. Identify someone who fits this description of an everyday hero and tell the person's story and why you think the person deserves to be recognized as a hero. (possible connections: *The Odyssey, The Hunger Games,* The *Hobbit,* or *The Color Purple*)
- Perhaps we all know (or have heard about) someone who has made a terrible mistake that has led to many difficulties, perhaps including financial disaster or physical suffering. Tell this person's story and reflect on how avoidable the source of the trouble was and about the factors that contributed to the person's bad experience (possible connections: *King Lear, Macbeth*).

A teacher might allow students to write for ten to fifteen minutes about the prompt. Then the teacher could ask students to share what they had written. If there are several contributions to the sharing, students might recognize a pattern of responses: for example, that some conscientious persons might break a rule or a law after they have exhausted all other options in an effort to accomplish a general benefit for others; a rather meek and humble person might find the resolve and courage to overcome difficult challenges in an effort to help others; that many complicating factors might add to a person's poor decision that leads to a downfall.

A student's sharing of a story can prompt other students to comment critically about the behavior of characters and the chance factors that influence the course of someone's life. This simple process of writing, sharing, and reflecting can tap into students' prior knowledge related to an assigned reading. This activation of prior knowledge is enough in itself to prepare learners to process a narrative and make critical judgments about the characters and the implications of the story as a whole.

THINKING THEMATICALLY: SURVEYS AND OPINIONNAIRES

Most teachers are familiar with the use of anticipation guides to introduce a work of literature. The guide would be a list of statements to which students respond as either true or false. As the name reveals, the intended use of the guide is to *anticipate* the matter of a text, whether it is a nonfiction text or a fiction narrative. Related possibilities for pre-reading are surveys or opinionnaires. The format includes a series of statements to which learners respond, perhaps with yes or no, or on a multipoint scale. It is easy to imagine a teacher presenting students with a set of statements about marriage as part of preparation for reading Kate Chopin's "The Story of an Hour" or *The Awakening*.

An example of such a survey appears below. A common process requires students to respond to the survey independently at first, then share their answers and the reasoning behind their answers in small groups. After small group discussion, the teacher can take a quick poll on the responses and then focus whole class discussion on the items on which there appears to be the most disagreement. These areas of disagreement represent the areas about which a group of learners need to have a conversation in order to consider possibilities and refine their thinking. The point isn't to discover conclusions that the teacher endorses but to become aware of a critical position from which to judge characters and an author's implications.

ANTICIPATION SURVEY: THE BONDS OF MATRIMONY

Directions: For each of the following statements, respond on this scale: 4 = strongly agree; 3 = agree; 2 = disagree; 1 = strongly disagree. After you have made your judgment, think of an example from your own experience (i.e., observing, reading, viewing) that supports or illustrates your decision.

Share your responses with a classmate, and try to come to an agreement about the extent to which any marriage is a mutually beneficial bond between two persons. When you are ready to share your decisions with the rest of the class, you should be able to express a generalization and support it by citing an example and explaining what the example shows.

_____ 1. Ideally, in a marriage, two people, in a sense, "become one."
_____ 2. Historically, men typically gain most benefits from marriage.
_____ 3. Marriage is not an idyllic state, but requires a lifetime of work to maintain the relationship.
_____ 4. As Shakespeare says, marriage is a union of "true minds," meaning that the bond is deeper than a mere physical attraction.
_____ 5. The loss of a spouse would be emotionally devastating.
_____ 6. While the loss of a loved one can be emotionally wrenching, it can also be liberating.
_____ 7. Anyone who finds joy in the loss of a relative is self-centered and emotionally cold.

_____ 8. Marriage, even a "good" one, necessarily means the loss of freedom for both partners.
_____ 9. Part of the beauty of marriage is the surrendering of part of one's liberty in order to form a union with someone else.
_____ 10. The appropriate response to the return of a missing loved one would be happiness.

Write a response to the following statement: *In any marriage, one person benefits most and the other partner probably seeks more freedom, or at least more choices about the matters that affect the couple.*

A teacher can anticipate a variety of responses to the survey and to the prompt that follows it. Some students will offer idealistic views of marriage, while other hold pessimistic views. Some students will recognize built-in inequities in any relationship but see mutual benefits in the end. Most students are likely to expect partners to be supportive of each other, even when the relationship is difficult. Students may begin the reading of a narrative with assumptions about the ways that individuals subordinate their own needs and preferences in bending to the will of another. In a good way for dialogue, the assumptions can cause a productive jolt when learners enter the text.

IMAGINING EXPERIENCE

Another useful preparation for the reading of a complex literary text involves discussions about problem-based scenarios. First, problem-based scenarios are useful for teachers who want to hone their skills at facilitating discussions, largely because truly problematic scenarios do not have easy solutions, requiring the teacher and learners to explore many options (McCann, 2003). In some instances, discussions about a set of scenarios can help students to define a core abstract concept, such as *hero* or *tragedy* (Johannessen, Kahn, & Walter, 2009). As part of the process of defining an abstract concept, thinkers express a set of criteria that can serve as a critical framework for reflecting on the events of a narrative and the behavior of characters.

Two examples follow. The first is a single scenario that can initiate a discussion about concepts about *justice*. The second example is a pair of scenarios that introduce discussion about the assumptions about *equity* and *accommodations*.

School Scenario

As Ruth exits the bus when it arrives at Floodrock High School, someone behind her gives her a shove that causes her to stumble and drop her books into the snow. When Ruth looks back, she sees Naomi grinning at her. As Naomi and her friends exit the bus, they point at Ruth and laugh. Since the beginning of the school year, Naomi has been harassing Ruth—by tossing food at her in the cafeteria, by spreading nasty rumors about her boyfriend, by threatening her in the hallways. On these occasions, Ruth's friends have asked her, "Are you going to put up with this stuff?" As Ruth bends down to retrieve her books from the snow, Naomi slaps her across the top of the head. Ruth has known Naomi for years, and Ruth knows that with little effort she can beat up her tormentor. If Ruth beats Naomi upon this occasion, the adult personnel outside of school are sure to witness the altercation. Ruth also knows that if she were to beat Naomi up at this moment, she would get in equal trouble with the dean, which probably means a suspension, even though Naomi was the one who started the trouble. From inside the bus, Ruth's friends watch her see what she will do in response to Naomi's abuse, fully expecting her to retaliate as a matter of honor.

From the Floodrock High School Handbook: *Any student involved in fighting in school or anywhere on school grounds, whether an initiator or a responder, will be subject to the following: 5-day, out-of-school suspension; referral to local police for possible criminal charges; and referral to the school's intervention and counseling process.*

Questions

What do you think Ruth should do? On what grounds do you base your recommendation?

If Ruth responds to Naomi by physically attacking her, what do you think the dean should do? If you were the dean, what action would you take with Ruth and Naomi? What principles would guide your decision?

Procedures:

Talk to two or three of your classmates about the scenario. Whenever you hear any observation that sounds like a rule or principle, write it down so that you can report your conclusions and analysis and so that you have these notes available for writing a composition.

After you have had a chance to talk about the scenario with partners, be prepared to share your conclusions and analysis with the rest of the class.

As you can imagine, many students recognize the scenario as a common experience that occurs in school—an experience that students find essentially unjust. Students appreciate the frustration of an adolescent who is the victim of repeated harassment and who faces possible disciplinary action for responding to the harassment. The discussion about the appropriate response from the victim's perspective and from the dean's perspective can help students to tap into their conceptions of *justice*: basic principles for just action, repairs for hurtful and criminal acts, and distinctions between justice and revenge. A teacher can well imagine how such discussion can be productive preparation for reading such texts as Barbara Kingsolver's *The Bean Trees*, Richard Wright's *Native Son*, *Merchant of Venice*, or *The Tempest*.

In a similar way, the following set of scenarios can help students to activate prior knowledge about equity and accommodations. The problem-based scenarios are likely to initiate rich discussions to help students to express principles for treating others equitably. The scenarios invite questions about the extent to which others need to alter their behavior or a whole environment in order to include someone else who seeks to be recognized as a member of a community. Such discussions are likely to make students aware of their own critical positions regarding complicated thematic questions. Discussions can help students to test their tentative conclusions and form a logical basis for their positions rather than stubbornly recite preconceived assumptions. Such dialogic activities will introduce thematic questions rather than narrow the possibilities for reading a text critically.

A reliable routine is for students to read the two scenarios on their own before discussing their judgments with a partner or a team of collaborators. It is useful to ask students to write down their conclusions and rationale in their notes or to post on an online discussion forum for the whole class to see. The small group discussion is key to involving everyone in the dialogue and prepares all participants for a large group conversation about the rights of individuals and any responsibilities for honoring group norms or preferences.

Two Scenarios: Individual Rights and Group Responsibilities

Scenario #1: Rosalyn's sister-in-law Betty and her family are coming to visit Rosalyn and her husband Lester and stay with them for three days in their home in Smyrna, Georgia. Now that her children are grown and independent, Rosalyn's home is spacious, with three guest bedrooms. There is plenty of room for Betty and her family. Here is the problem: Betty's husband Jethro has a deathly allergy to legumes, which would include peanuts. Even the smell or sight of peanuts makes him nauseous. The town of Smyrna is deep in the heart of peanut-growing country. Lester loves peanuts, and there are usually bowls of peanuts set about the house. Many of Rosalyn's and Lester's favorite recipes contain peanuts. Five years ago, Rosalyn and Lester's daughter Suellen was third runner-up to the queen of the "Goober Festival" in Smyrna. Pictures of Suellen from the festival parade abound throughout the house. In some cases, the photos capture Suellen in front of a peanut-shaped float from the Goober Festival Parade. If Jethro is going to have a comfortable stay in Rosalyn's home, she and Lester will have to make some changes, or send Betty, Lester, and their family to stay at the Brer Rabbit motel fifteen minutes away. What accommodations, if any, would be reasonable for Rosalyn and Lester to make? On what basis would you make these recommendations? Should they keep their home and customary practices as they have always been and send the visitors to a motel? Explain.

Scenario #2: Administrators from Oak Forest High School were aware that a current eighth grader with a serious latex allergy would be entering the high school in the next academic year. Garland Bradford, the eighth grader, is deathly allergic to latex. As an example, consider that latex balloons commonly seen to celebrate birthdays at the school could pop, triggering the aerosol spread of proteins that could cause Garland to go into shock. When Garland enters Oak Forest High School, the enrollment will be just over 3,000 students. In anticipation of Garland's entry to the high school, the administration has instituted a systematic removal of all latex. This means that balloons are banned. Students are forbidden from using latex erasers. The swim team has replaced their latex swim caps with more expensive synthetic caps. The school nurse will replace latex gloves with synthetic gloves in her office. Administrators have advised all students that they should avoid wearing any clothing that includes latex. To what extent have administrators gone too far in trying to change the behavior of more than 3,000 students and staff in order to accommodate one student? On what principles do you base your judgment? Should Garland receive instruction at home or some other protected environment rather than have thousands accommodate him? On what principles do you base your judgment?

You can well imagine how discussion about the two scenarios will put learners in a good position for their own dialogue about Ellison's *Invisible Man*, Cather's *My Antonia*, Keyes' *Flowers for Algernon*, Beals' *Warrior Don't Cry*, or Hurst's "The Scarlet Ibis." Such preparatory discussions do not reveal the plot and thus spoil the reading experience, nor do they preclude students' drawing their own conclusions about the implications of the narrative. Instead, the preliminary dialogue is likely to motivate students to read, help them to follow the narrative, and reflect critically on its implications.

As noted above, scenarios are useful instructional tools to foster lively discussions that can be valuable in themselves and that serve to offer a point of entry into thinking critically about a complex text. In addition to the three sample scenarios above, teachers can find similar scenarios in many publications (Smagorinsky, McCann, & Kern, 1987; McCann, 2003, McCann, Johannessen, Kahn, & Flanagan, 2006; Johannessen, Kahn, & Walter, 1982; Johannessen, Kahn, & Walter, 2009; McCann, D'Angelo, Galas, & Greska, 2015). But any teacher would want the flexibility to construct her own set of scenarios. Here are a few guidelines for writing scenarios to spark classroom discussion:

The scenario is a brief narrative, so it should have the basic elements of any compelling story: distinct characters, a specific setting or context, a core conflict, and possible complicating factors.

The central character of the scenario should be someone that the reader can care about, whether that attention is critical or supportive.

The central conflict should be debatable, so write the scenario in a way that does not invite a response that all readers are likely to share.

The central conflict should seem consequential to students.

The questions about the scenario should invite analysis and not a simple yes or no response.

COMPLICATED CASES AND COMPLEX TEXTS

A case is simply a more developed scenario. In some instances, instead of discussing a series of scenarios, it is useful to delve into a more complicated situation. Malcolm Gladwell (2005) reports that humans make quick judgments about others, and our hasty judgments are often right. Of course, when our presumptions are inaccurate, misperception can lead to tragic, and sometimes deadly, results. The following case involves making judgments about a character. The process raises subsequent questions about perceptions: How reliable are our perceptions of other people? How do we know people are who we think they are?

Perception of others is complicated, as history shows. The friendly neighbor, like humble auto assembly worker John Demjanjuk, turns out to have been a vicious Nazi concentration camp guard, or a respected member of the clergy hides some dark deeds. In our daily lives, we might encounter people who clearly are trying to deceive us and perhaps we turn a blind eye to the shortcomings of others who attract us for various reasons. Readers encounter these same problems in literature, especially when a narrator reveals some details and conceals others or puts us in a position to fall victim to our own prejudices.

A teacher can present the case below as a simulation/role-playing activity. The activity has three key elements: a narrative that introduces a problem, a data set to support problem solving, and descriptions of possible viewpoints for examining the central problem in many ways. The role playing will require small group preparation, and a teacher would have to manage a discussion forum. The following case is an invention, but teachers can find debatable cases of all sorts in the news. The case below can serve as a template for teachers to construct their own activities, inventing problem-based narratives that can spark critical thinking that serves students as they enter a literary text. See McCann (2014) or McCann, Kahn, and Walter (2018) for guidance in how to construct case studies and simulation role-playing activities.

SAMPLE CASE: "WHO *IS* THIS GUY?"

When Mr. and Mrs. Jennings met their daughter Wendy's new boyfriend, they were impressed that he seemed like a nice, quiet, polite, and steady young man. Wendy's romantic interest is named Bobby Cashman, but his friends call him B.D. He does not seem very ambitious, but he has a steady job as a librarian in the law library at Middle Border State University.

While the relationship between Wendy, now a kindergarten teacher, and B.D. seems to have become progressively serious, the Jennings have begun to have some doubts that they really know who B.D. is. They know that he sings, plays guitar, and performs on weekends with a blues band called the Urban Blues Breakers; but this activity has seemed to the Jennings to be a harmless avocation that would pass with time. Then neighbors alerted the Jennings that they had heard B.D.'s band play at a local club called the Chessboard Lounge and were taken aback by the lyrics of the songs he sang and the general image that B.D. projected from the stage. Simply put, B.D. projected a drug-addicted, dangerous, and renegade image, singing songs about getting drunk, gambling, fleeing arrest, and abusing women. He dressed all in black and wore dark glasses. He seemed contemptuous toward the audience and angry with his band members.

Crimes and Suspicions: To complicate B.D.'s image, it seems that some current crimes in the community matched some of the lyrics in B.D.'s songs, as if he were openly confessing his complicity in the crimes. In addition, the news reports about the crimes offer the description of an offender that looks very similar to B.D. (See the attached lyrics and news story.)

Question for Discussion: *Who is B.D. (Bobby) Cashman, really?* This is an important question for Mr. and Mrs. Jennings, because they would do everything they can to protect their daughter from involvement in a potentially catastrophic relationship. So, the conclusions about B.D. will help the Jennings to answer these questions: *Should they try to prevent their daughter Wendy from a romantic entanglement with B.D.? What would be the parents' justification for interfering? How could they ever prevent her from seeing B.D. if she is an adult and can make her own decisions? Should Wendy defer to her parents' cautions and wishes?*

Points of View: What would each person have to say about B.D.? How would they answer the questions that the Jennings are struggling with? Each team will present the arguments and insights from the point of view of one of the following characters.

Cloris Miriam, Ph.D. (Supervisor at the MBSU Law Library): Cloris is Bobby's immediate supervisor at the Middle Border State University Law Library. Cloris thinks B.D. is great and does not have many bad comments about him. She has never heard of him being called B.D. and only addresses him as Bobby. In fact, she would be confused by anyone else's references to him as B.D. She is pleased by his work performance and is pleased overall to have him on her team. She has never had any extended conversation with him, outside of their work-related communications. Occasionally, Bobby has shown up late to work looking disheveled, but this does not happen often. She has noticed that he seems to have a deep interest in criminal law and has been known during lunch and breaks to read about criminal cases related to violent crimes. In the end, he is a rather quiet, steady, and reliable employee.

Theresa Waters (Owner/Manager of the Chessboard Lounge): Theresa has hired B.D. and his band to perform regularly at her Chessboard Lounge. She is disappointed by the accusations that B.D. could be involved in criminal activities, although she is not entirely surprised. She would describe him as a collected and balanced person off stage. He seems to be passionate about his craft and is what she considers an above-average musical artist. His attire when he is at the lounge is quite dedicated to his on-stage character: dark, troubled, and menacing. Unlike most of the musicians she has hired for her club, she has not had any extended conversation with B.D., but she does know one thing for sure—his edgy performance draws a reasonably big crowd and business for her lounge.

Mickey Bloomfield (B.D.'s neighbor): Mickey is actually a nickname for Michelle Bloomfield, a retiree who lives in the same old apartment building where B.D. lives. In her retirement, Mickey has plenty of time to observe the comings and goings of her neighbors in the apartment building. She frequently encounters B.D. as he is on his way to another blues gig at a local club. When asked about B.D., she always scoffs and complains, "That boy is up to no good!" She is ready to share that he is always in and out of his apartment at all hours of the night and constantly brings strange, suspicious-looking people home with him. She warns Wendy's parents that B.D. has a toxic lifestyle and will inevitably be a bad influence on their daughter. She believes that Wendy needs to date an "upstanding citizen" and not some "dead-beat kid."

William ("Wide Willie") Bishop (a member of the Urban Blues Breakers): Despite his name, William is actually a tall, lanky fellow. He adopted the name Wide Willie because it sounded like a classic bluesman name. He grew up in an affluent family, but he never went to college.

When asked about B.D., he insists that B.D.'s stage appearance is all an act, just as the name "Wide Willie" is part of an invented persona. According to Willie, B.D. actually cares deeply about the band and all of its members, but he does get frustrated when things do not go perfectly during performances. Willie once suggested changing the name of the band to "Wide Willie and the Wailers," but B.D. flew into a rage about the suggestion, insisting that it was *his* band. Willie observes that B.D. chooses to live simply and does not want a "big fancy job" that might absorb too much of his time, which is why he keeps his regular job at the law library, where he has limited responsibilities. Willie insists that people only know what they see on stage, but in reality, he is a pretty sensitive guy. His song lyrics reflect his passion for correcting the wrongs of the world, which is why he often writes about current crimes. From what Willie has observed, B.D. is "head-over-heels for Wendy" and "would never do anything to hurt her."

Wendy: She has trouble understanding her parents' concerns or skepticism. She knows Bobby to be kindhearted and pleasant offstage and is just projecting a bluesman persona onstage. She judges that his music isn't her favorite but she loves his personality when they are together. There is no way that he could have done the criminal acts that people suspect him of. He is a contrast with the stage persona and the descriptions of a criminal suspect. Just last week he bought Wendy a beautiful necklace that she had admired. When Wendy asked him where he got the money for it, he just said he got lucky gambling. Wendy realizes that no one would drop that kind of money on someone he didn't really like. But Wendy also knows that he failed to return money he borrowed from her a few weeks ago.

Dr. Thomas Rizza (a psychologist friend of the family): Dr. Rizza recognizes that this is a difficult situation that the Jennings find themselves in. He has done research about identity formation and has studied B.D. Cashman specifically. He has listened to his music, analyzed the lyrics, and visited the clubs during his performances on several occasions. It seems that his stage persona is a large part of the performance element that is part of the music industry. Dr. Rizza is not confident that B.D. is the poor, humble individual that he would like the Jennings to believe him to be. Dr. Rizza has watched Wendy and B.D. together at family functions. They appear to be normal and well-adjusted, and there exist no warning signs of abuse based upon their physical and verbal interactions. According to Dr. Rizza, there appears to be little connection between what B.D. does on stage and how he acts as a human being off stage. At the same time, he cautions that Wendy probe into his true character, because if he is that good at acting onstage, it wouldn't be a big step to disguise many aspects of his personality, which compromises their relationship.

TALKING ABOUT THE CASE

Small Group Preparation: You and your partners will have approximately twenty minutes to create the responses that your group believes an assigned character would give to the Jennings' questioning. You and your group members should be able to answer the question, "Who is B.D. (Bobby) Cashman?" You have the freedom to decide if Bobby is good or bad, but you must offer evidence and reasoning to support the position you choose. After you have had sufficient time to prepare, your group should select a group member to assume the character and represent that character during the large group discussion.

Large Group Forum: The Jennings have decided to hold an intervention for Wendy to confront her about her relationship. Each character from the "Points of View" list has been asked to attend. Each participant will offer a view of Bobby to argue for or against his continued relationship with Wendy. Dr. Rizza, the psychologist, will lead the discussion. Those members who are not acting as a character are allowed to send notes and advice to their actors to help them maintain a strong argument as the intervention goes on.

Debriefing: After each character has had an opportunity to "speak" his or her mind, the entire class will come together to judge B.D.'s (Bobby's) character and to decide how to advise Wendy. The group discussion will help you to develop the arguments that you will need in order to be prepared to write to Wendy's parents with your advice.

Information (Data) about the Case: The following information might help you in thinking about the case. The artifacts include the lyrics to a blue song composed by B.D. Cashman. The news report describes a fatal shooting, perpetrated by someone who loosely fits the description of B.D. Cashman.

Flat-Out Emergent Self Blues
B.D. Cashman

Just yesterday mornin' I discovered who I am:
So familiar with meanness, there's no denying.
Just yesterday mornin' I saw for sure who I am:
Can't be denying the meanness inside me.

You were once my lovin' woman, but
I couldn't give enough to keep you satisfied.
Now instead of tryin' to love and hug ya'
I came home today to show I'm needy, too.

I learned my father was a killer,
And maybe I'm another one, too.

You mind what you're doin' now
Or my born meanness will come to you.

Just yesterday mornin' I discovered who I am:
So familiar with meanness, there's no denying.
Just yesterday mornin' I saw for sure who I am:
Can't be denying the meanness inside me.
Can't be denying the meanness inside me.

"Shooting in Brainard Park," reported in the City Times-Courier

Two men were shot, one fatally, during an incident that city police detective Robert Jenkins described as "a drug deal gone bad." The shooting occurred in the Brainard Park neighborhood of the city, on Tuesday night. The victims were meeting someone to sell drugs when they were approached by two men, one of whom opened fire. A witness reported to detective Jenkins that the gunman was a white man who wore a black leather jacket and dark glasses. He appeared to have a tattoo on his neck, but the witness could not describe the details of the tattoo. The gunman and his accomplice remain at large.

Discussions about such a case immerse students in procedures for judging how they perceive others, especially when conflicting reports complicate the efforts to understand a character. Many novels put readers in a similar position. Here are just a few: Austen's *Pride and Prejudice* or *Emma*, Fitzgerald's *The Great Gatsby*, Cormier's *I Am the Cheese*, Myers' *Monster*, or any book in the Harry Potter series. In addition to the value of such activities as preparation for critical reading, the procedures involve students in extensive discussion, elaborated writing, and close reading of testimonies and a verse text. Students find such preparatory activities engaging, and the activities help teachers to connect reading, writing, speaking, and listening as reciprocal language experiences.

POSSIBILITIES AND CAUTIONS

Some ill-conceived pre-reading activities do nothing constructive to prepare students to read a text closely and critically. Regrettably, some preparatory activities undermine the experience of reading a narrative by narrowly focusing attention or revealing elements of the plot. As reported in an earlier text (McCann & Knapp, 2021), when a teacher has carefully constructed activities, pre-reading can invite students into a text, especially one that might otherwise seem too daunting to tackle, and can involve learners in analytical procedures that transfer to their work with literature. The summary below (see table 2.1) suggests the various purposes for pre-reading and the possible learning structures that can help to prepare readers for their encounters with a text.

YOUR VIEW

You and your colleagues may have some skepticism about the use of pre-reading activities, especially in the later years of high school. In some instances, teachers worry that the pre-reading will co-opt the actual reading experience. Other teachers see the playfulness of a simulation role-playing activity as frivolous and time-consuming. As with any instructional practice, it is useful to have a firm research and theory grounding for activities intended for preparing students for their reading. Toward this end, you might find it informative to discuss with peers their judgments about the potentialities and cautions for relying on pre-reading activities. The following questions will be useful to explore.

Table 2.1 Pre-Reading Activities and Their Function

Activity Structure	Function/Goal
Anticipation guide	Activates schema
	Supports the making of predictions
Journal writing and discussion	Activates prior knowledge
	Suggests a focus for reading and discussion
	Equips learners with a critical lens
	Serves as an informal assessment
Team research	Builds relevant background knowledge
	Provides a biographical and historical lens for reading
	Suggests a focus for reading
Survey/opinionnaire	Fosters critical thinking about thematic implications
	Positions readers to make inferences on many levels
	Defines a key concept
Ranking	Develops a critical lens for reading
	Refines a definition of a key concept
Scenarios	Generates an extended definition of a key concept
	Fosters an empathic response to the characters
Case study	Develops a critical framework
	Anticipates problems and themes
	Fosters an empathic response to the characters
Simulation/role-playing	Develops a critical framework
	Anticipates problems and themes
	Fosters an empathic response to the characters
Writing a narrative	Anticipates the structure of a narrative
	Anticipates thematic explorations

1. What value, if any, do you see in pre-reading activities?
2. What specific kinds of pre-reading activities seem to you to be the most promising? How did you arrive at this decision?
3. How would you distinguish between an unproductive or ill-conceived pre-reading activity and one that can prepare and motivate students for reading a complex text?
4. What cautions would you offer a colleague about how to use pre-reading activities or about using them at all?

Chapter 3

What We Notice and How We Construct Meaning

We acknowledge the influence of the work of Michael Smith and Jeff Wilhelm (2010) in suggesting an instructional sequence that meets students where they live (in popular culture) by introducing a graphic image as the basis for practicing a discipline of reading literary texts. The sequence of practice continues with a simple or constructed text and then moves forward with shared inquiry into a more complex text. In this chapter, we illustrate this sequence by beginning with a drawing from *The New Yorker*, applying derived rules of notice and signification to constructed texts, and then applying the principles to more complex texts. Of course, a teacher might draw from any number of images or clips from movies or sitcoms to talk about how viewers can tell when to read a text as ironic.

As we have noted in a previous book (McCann & Knapp, 2021), one particularly difficult challenge for readers is to recognize ironic tone and then note the implications of the irony. Even in the world of politics, leaders sometimes express what seem to be outrageous ideas and then defend themselves by noting that they were speaking ironically or writing ironically and journalists and critics have failed to detect the obvious tone. "Can't you take a joke?" the provocative speaker might ask. For students who are asked to write about their interpretations of texts, explaining how irony and satire work is especially tricky. In some ways, the interpretation is like explaining a joke: you might simply "get it" but find it difficult to explain to others. So, detecting irony and explaining its implications are challenges both for reading texts and for writing about texts.

AN INSTRUCTIONAL SEQUENCE: SHARED INQUIRY AND PURPOSEFUL PRACTICE

As an example of how teachers can help adolescents to define rules for noticing elements of narratives and determining the significance of these text features we offer a sequence that allows students practice with working with ironic texts. These are examples drawn from our own experience and from the experience of high school teachers, including former students who teach in high schools.

We begin by displaying a drawing from the cover of a 2017 issue of *The New Yorker*. The drawing from R. Kikuo Johnson is titled "Tech Support" (see figure 3.1). In introducing the drawing, we note our intention to discover how to distinguish between literal and ironic reading of a text. The dialogic effort, then, is to identify rules for reading ironic texts that students can apply to other texts and use for sharing their interpretations. We offer the drawing below, followed by a bit of dialogue from the classroom.

Figure 3.1 **R. Kikuo Johnson.** "Tech Support." *The New Yorker, October 23, 2017, the work is reprinted by permission of R. Kikuo Johnson,* ©R. Kikuo Johnson.

Ms. Shannon: When I saw this cover on *The New Yorker*, I showed it to a friend and said, "Don't you think that's funny?" But after studying the picture for a couple of minutes, he said, "What's funny about it? I find it terrifying!" We talked about it for a while, and it dawned on me that the drawing can be both funny and terrifying. I am interested in knowing what you think, and, more importantly, how you figured it out. How do you know that this isn't simply a report about the way things are on the streets of Manhattan in 2017?

Gabi: Well, you know that that can't be true. You know that there aren't like robots walking around like that.

Dan: Why not? Didn't you ever see the videos from Google showing robots monitoring social distancing and robots fighting to get out of a room? That could happen.

Ms. Shannon: So, Dan, you are saying that we can read the drawing as a report of the way things are now?

Dan: Not exactly, but robots are getting more and more like human beings and doing jobs that humans usually do.

Val: But the picture shows that the robots have taken over. It's not like Google showing off their robots. It's like an exaggeration. Like the robots have replaced the humans.

Ms. Shannon: This probably seems obvious to you, but where do you see exaggeration?

Clifford: The whole thing is exaggerated. There are mostly robots, even a robot dog. But there is just one human and one real dog.

Stephanie: The robots are doing stuff that humans normally do.

Ms. Shannon: Like what?

Stephanie: The robots are like rushing off to work and stuff. One of the robots is carrying a cup of coffee, like a robot would need coffee.

Desi: And one of the robots is dialing a cell phone. That seems strange to me, because the robot is already a machine. They would probably already build in some kind of smart phone and it wouldn't need a separate phone.

Karen: One of the robots is walking a robot dog, like it has to walk outside to go to the bathroom or to get some exercise.

Ms. Shannon: All right, so you are noticing at least three features of the drawing. One is that there is *exaggeration*. In this case, it is that the robots have taken over. I hope that is an exaggeration and we are not quite there yet. The other element that you noticed is that some things are the opposite of the way they normally are: there is a kind of *reversal*, with the robots doing human activities. You also pointed out some things that seem illogical, like walking a robot dog or a robot dialing a cell phone. We might call this an *incongruity*. So, you are pointing to three elements or patterns: *exaggeration*, *reversal*, and *incongruity*.

Clifford: And the human looks like a homeless guy begging for money. And the dog is a real dog that looks sort of scared or confused.

Gabi: And the robot is not giving the homeless guy money, but like a washer or gear, whatever you call it. That would be something that the robot thinks is valuable, but the guy is looking like "What is that for?"

Ms. Shannon: That's interesting. You said that the robot "thinks." Is that what you mean?

Gabi: You know what I mean. That robot is like assuming that the guy would value the same thing.

Dan: It's like artificial intelligence. It's like functioning the way it was programmed, but it's also learning, so like it "thinks." Yeah.

Ms. Shannon: To go back to where I began, when you put everything together, what do you think the drawing means? What is the artist implying? I see some hands up now, but I would like you to talk this over in your groups. I am interested in hearing your full analysis, not just a conclusion. So here is the focus for your group discussion: *What is the artist implying with the drawing, and how did you figure out these implications?*

Through this dialogic process, students are discovering what they notice when they look at a text and determine that it is not to be read literally but ironically. The teacher helps the students to find the language to label the text features that the students notice. The text features that the students noticed in this instance—exaggeration, reversal, and incongruity—are common to irony and satire. As the discussion progresses in the small group meetings and the subsequent sharing of the groups' analyses, the teacher can help students to transform the observed tendencies into rules for noticing ironic tone and interpreting it.

Although the process of inquiry and discovery may seem painstaking and time-consuming to many teachers, the dialogue is usually engaging and enjoyable for students. Furthermore, the emphasis is on the *procedures* for interpreting rather than the recall of information that a teacher might present about how to read irony. When students become aware of the procedures for identifying ironic tone and interpreting an ironic text, the learning is *generative*, in the sense that students can apply the procedures to other texts, and therefore the command of the procedures generates other learning.

EXPANDING AND VARYING DISCUSSION

In spring 2020, we found ourselves in a situation where the only discussions we could have with students were online. The discussion that we reproduce below was part of an extended online discussion forum with university students. Although the language and level of elaboration are far more mature than a teacher could expect from a high school class, the process would be similar with younger adolescents. The dialogic principles remain the same:

- Post a discussion prompt that does not have a prespecified answer, inviting everyone to contribute.
- Specify the expectation that students will not only post a response to the prompt, but they will reply to a classmate's comments.
- The teacher monitors the discussion to react to students' posts. Students, after all, want to know that the teacher cares enough to read what they have written. The reactions might be further questions to extend and refine the dialogue.
- The teacher looks for the general trends across the discussion forum and offers a summary of the conclusions the class seems to have reached. With this sharing, the teacher invites students to add, refine, or question the summary statements.

The first step is to initiate discussion with an open-ended prompt. Here are the prompts we used:

- If I read "Tech Support" literally, I would have to say that robots (and their mechanical pets) have assumed dominion over human society. Read as a report, R. Kikuo Johnson's drawing asserts that this is the situation now. How can you read the drawing any other way?
- To many readers of "Tech Support," it is obviously ironic. But what makes it ironic? What features of the image did the illustrator/author (R. Kikuo Johnson) expect an audience to recognize (i.e., notice) to know that the drawing is intended to be ironic? What are the features of the drawing that allow you to read it as ironic? If it is ironic, what meaning do you derive? How can you explain to someone else how you can reasonably construct this meaning?

The following excerpt comes from an extended discussion thread initiated from the prompts. We have indicated in bold italics where students have expressed rules about what to notice and about how to read narratives generally. In reviewing the discussion forum as a whole, we were able to draw on these generalizations, sometimes repeated by other students, as a means for summarizing the discussion and formalizing the procedures for detecting and interpreting irony.

Katie Torres: You can tell the illustrator wants the picture to be ironic, because he has the ***robots doing common human activities*** such as drinking coffee, walking a robot dog, and looking on a phone. By switching the roles of robots and humans, the illustrator conveys the message that most humans are functioning in their day-to-day lives as robots. . . . . The actual human is the main ***conflict*** in the picture. His presence as a homeless person reveals the lack of emotions the robots have since most of them can walk by him without even stopping.

Jaemee Cordero: When we think of that term, we think how technology helps us in a variety of ways: Q&A Forums, people fixing computers, Google . . . And yet, the drawing is *more exaggerated*. It presents technology "supporting" a human by giving a beggar some gears or perhaps what is considered monetary in this world.

Jeff Jakubik: . . . *many movies these days* that feature robots are created in a way that builds sympathy for them. They show that these robots have human characteristics, and then if something bad happens to them, the audience feels sorry for them.

Matthew Wolkober: The robots texting, walking robot dogs, drinking coffee, and using a tool kit as a work bag is in *direct contrast* to the homeless human and his dog who are receiving cogs as coins.

Autumn South: The irony is also pushed by having a human, which represents *the creator of the robots*, sitting down in the corner, obviously struggling and/or *homeless, and begging for money* (from the machines that humans created).

Sam Panek: The main feature that shows this image is supposed to be ironic is that the "people" walking by are *robots that are doing human-like actions*. Rather than giving the homeless man change, one robot gives him gears and washers. Along with this, one of the robots is holding a coffee cup in its hand while walking, which can also symbolize irony since robots would not be drinking coffee to begin with. There is another robot on a cellphone, and finally a robot walking his robot dog.

Amori Love: The irony that I see in the picture is that the *robots are living like we do*, bustling to work, guzzling coffee down as they run late, and even to the extent of having a pet. Kikuo Johnson did not accidentally include a robot walking a robotic dog; the *dog is even the same color as the living breathing one* illustrated.

Amanda De La O: Within the drawing, the artist incorporates robots who seem to be part of the active labor force, going to work, drinking coffee, and walking their robotic dogs, while the only human in the cartoon is sitting off to the side begging for "money." At first glance, the robot with the phone stood out to me as being the epitome of irony because *I would never expect a robot to need a phone*...

The discussion continued for several turns online. In fact, there were sixteen participants and thirty-three posts. But even within the selected excerpt, we could see that students were stating generalizations that can be expressed as rules for noticing and interpreting. We were able to pull out these rules from the students' posts and summarize the trends in their observations. Here is a portion of our email summary:

Dear Students,

Thank you for your very thoughtful contributions to the discussion about "Tech Support." From your comments, I have pulled out a few "rules" for reading ironic texts:

- The **title** continues to hold a privileged place. We need to notice the title and its connection to the rest of the text. This is a beginning place for noticing and constructing meaning.
- Notice the **reversals** of situations and behaviors as we normally expect to see them.
- Notice **contrasts**, **contradictions**, or **incongruities**.
- Notice **exaggerations**, including **overstatement** and **understatement**.
- Notice **parodies**: imitations of common scenes in a comical or subversive way.

These are all indicators of irony. The selected quotes offer the bases for these rules. I appreciated everyone's contributions, and I especially enjoyed your reactions to your peers' comments. In some cases, you have noted where the interpretations of others have expanded your views of the text. This seems to be an ideal outcome of discussion. If you have any suggestions for additions, deletions, or refinements to these rules, please let me know or share your thoughts with the rest of the class.

This summary is necessary to help students to be aware of the rules they derived as a group. Our intention is to build on this awareness by planning for practice with conventional print texts. Not only is it sometimes tough for students to read texts as ironic, but it is especially hard for readers to *write about their interpretations* of ironic texts. As noted earlier, listeners or readers might recognize sarcasm and jokes in an instant, but it is difficult to explain to someone else how they know someone is being sarcastic or why a joke is funny. So, it is helpful to engage students in discovering "rules" for reading ironic texts. The rules can serve as *warrants* for explaining the significance of the features of the text that we can point to in supporting an interpretation. In writing about literature, it is not enough to cite details from the text, since different readers can construct different meanings from those same details. The writer needs to apply "rules" for reading to show how a particular meaning can be derived.

It is practically useless to lecture students on irony or to ask them to read a definition of *irony* or to commit the definition to memory. Instead, through an inquiry process that involves discussion, students can *construct an understanding* of irony, as students have demonstrated in their thoughtful interchanges, whether in the classroom or online.

ORCHESTRATING PURPOSEFUL PRACTICE

It is not sufficient to be able to recite rules for reading and interpreting an ironic text or other narratives. The key is for students to be able to apply consciously their procedures for working with a text and discussing it with other readers. As we have suggested in an earlier book (McCann & Knapp, 2021), it might be necessary for some groups of students to transition from the reading of a drawing from a popular magazine to the reading of a short, constructed text. In other instances, after a class has derived a set of rules for recognizing and interpreting irony and satire, the students may be ready to move immediately into a more complex text, as we discuss below.

For the purpose of illustration, one constructed text below shows how students might use a conventional print text to practice the procedures that they have learned from discussion about a visual image. The text is the creative product of Mike Segal, a teacher at Harriton High School, in Rosemont, Pennsylvania. Mike adapted the memo from a similar one distributed by a colleague during labor dispute at another high school. The instructional procedure would begin by distributing, posting, or projecting the text and asking the students to respond in small groups. The teacher might prompt discussion in this way: *I received this memo in my mailbox this morning. I didn't know if this is for real, or if one of my colleagues is playing a joke on me. If it is a joke, how can you tell for sure? And, if you are certain it is a joke, what is the point of it?*

The idea of the sequence is that once students have derived a set of rules or procedures for reading a certain type of text, they can practice with purpose by applying the procedures with another text. Their attempts at reading rely on discussion, involving the insights and reservations of others.

MEMO: REVISED STUDENT RESTROOM USE POLICY

FLOODROCK COMMUNITY HIGH SCHOOL

Floodrock, Illinois
  TO: All Teachers
  DATE: October 3
  SUBJECT: Revised Student Restroom Use Policy
  In the past, teachers have followed informal procedures for granting students restroom use. Teachers and other staff have reported that some students have been taking advantage of this privilege and have wasted valuable instructional time and have disrupted class as they returned to the classroom. Effective two weeks from today, teachers and students will follow a new policy to allow for more consistent accounting for students' restroom use and to ensure equal treatment for all students.

Under the new policy, a "Restroom Trip Bank" will be established for each student. The first day of each month, each student will be credited with fifteen trips in the "Bank." Restroom Trip credits can accumulate from month to month so that any unused credits from one month will carry over to the next month.

The entrances to the bathrooms throughout the school are being equipped with personnel identification stations and computer-linked voice recognition devices. Each student will provide to Maintenance two copies of voice prints (one normal and one under stress). The voice recognition will be operational but not restrictive for the first month. Students can acquaint themselves with the stations during this period and "train" the stations to recognize your voice.

When the system is fully operational, if a student's Restroom Trip Bank reaches zero, the doors to the bathroom will not unlock for that student until the next month, when the Bank has been refreshed. Under such circumstances, a student can appeal to one of the Deans for emergency use.

In addition, all restroom stalls are being equipped with timed paper roll retractors. If the stall is occupied for more than three minutes, an alarm will sound. Thirty seconds after the alarm sound, the roll of paper will retract into the wall, the toilet will flush, and the stall door will open. If the stall remains occupied, a picture (headshot only) will be taken.

The picture will then be posted on the digital message board in the Commons area. Anyone whose picture is displayed three times will receive an in-school suspension and parents will be notified.

If students have any questions about this policy, please direct them to their counselors.

Go Braves!

The discussion below is a composite drawn from many discussions about the text. This whole-class discussion follows from the small group work during which all students had an opportunity to react to the text—both by pointing to what they noticed and sharing the conclusions at which they have arrived about its implications.

Tim: When I read this, I thought this is exactly what the deans in this school would do. It is like a prison. You can't do anything around here.
Lizbeth: What they describe, that has to be illegal. Especially taking your picture in the stall. That's an invasion of privacy. They can't do that. So, that's an exaggeration, so you know it can't be real.

Joey: I think that deans would just say you can't use the restrooms. They wouldn't go to all the trouble and expense to keep track of how many times each student uses the restroom. But the voice recognition thing is cool. Maybe they could use that so someone doesn't have to sit at the door and check your ID every morning.

Mr. Segal: So, you are convinced that the memo isn't real and we don't have to follow the policy.

Chip: The idea of a bathroom bank is craaaazy.

Desiree: That would be cruel if you ran out of credit and you couldn't get in the bathroom anymore.

Mr. Segal: You are pointing to some exaggerations and some incongruities. So, what is the point of making this policy up and writing it in a memo.

Chip: There is no point. It is just supposed to be funny. It's a joke.

Joey: You probably wrote it yourself. It sort of says that the people who run the school are so controlling that they even want to control how often you use the restroom.

Lizbeth: They might not be saying that bathroom use is so out of hand that someone has to control it. But they are suggesting that the leaders and the teachers in the school like to control everything. A student might have made this up to freak everyone out, but there is something sort of true about it. You know that people want to control you.

Desiree: And it's disrespectful. I mean, it says that the people in charge are disrespectful. Different people have different needs for using the restroom. You shouldn't have to explain, and you shouldn't have someone count how many times you had to use the restroom. That's nobody's business. I know this is like made up, but it makes me so mad.

Mr. Segal: Maybe that's the point.

The exchange above shows students making judgments about a conventional print text by applying procedures similar to the ones they followed in constructing meaning about a graphic illustration. In working with the simple constructed text, students shared that they noticed that the descriptions of policy were probably exaggerated, that the proposed practice ran counter to the respectful behavior that students might expect, and that the new policy seemed improbable, even in a school that some students found prison-like. Once learners recognized these elements of the text, they could laugh at the absurdity but they could also question the purpose for writing and sharing such a memo and reflect on the implications for their school and for living within oppressive restrictions anywhere.

TRANSITIONING TO MORE COMPLEX TEXTS

Many teachers we have observed would have dismissed the preceding steps and moved immediately to a short story or novel. That is probably appropriate in many instances, but we find that if teachers want students to be aware of procedures of reading a complex literary text, the learners benefit from discussion-based activities that help readers to discover "rules" for noting and interpreting. After becoming aware of common text features and logical bases for constructing meaning based on the recognition of these features, learners can consciously put procedures to work with more complex expressions.

Several frequently anthologized short stories have ironic elements: Kate Chopin's "The Story of an Hour," Stephen Crane's "The Blue Hotel," Saki's "The Interlopers," Guy de Maupassant's "The Necklace," and Ring Lardner's "Haircut." As noted in an earlier book (McCann & Knapp, 2021), it is helpful to model for students what an experienced reader of literature notices, interrogates, anticipates, and reflects on when reading a literary text. In each case, the ironic effect is different; but for each story, the reader needs to reach the end in order to have a full sense of the irony. For the purpose of illustration, we focus here on Chopin's "The Story of an Hour."

At this point in the sequence, teachers would model for students how they are interacting with the story. Obviously, it can be tedious for students to listen at length to the teacher read and "think aloud." The teacher should read a few paragraphs, pausing frequently to reveal what she is thinking about and then ask students to pick up the reading and imitate what the teacher has been doing. This is essentially reciprocal teaching: observing the demonstration first and then imitating the model. Here is what such a demonstration might look like:

> *Mr. Victor:* The first thing I notice is that the title is "The Story of an Hour." I don't know if the action of the narrative takes place within an hour or if the story suggests what could happen within an hour's time for anyone. I just have to see. The author is Kate Chopin. I am not an expert on her life, but I know she is often identified as an early feminist writer. I know her husband died relatively young and she had to assume responsibility for managing the family's finances and continue for the care of her children. At the same time, I read that she had a deep affection for her husband, and one story about Kate Chopin had her climbing bareback on a horse to ride in search of a doctor when her husband fell seriously ill. This suggests to me that the marriage was generally a good one, and Chopin cared for her husband. So, let me read a bit of the story here: "Knowing that Mrs. Mallard was afflicted with a heart trouble, great care was taken to break to her as gently as possible the news of her husband's death." So, I think I should pay attention to the character's name, *Mallard*. What do you think the author expected us to notice about that?
>
> *Cliff:* That's a kind of duck. The kind that has the green head. You see them on ponds around here.

Mr. Victor: Why might the author name the character *Mallard*? I don't know much about ducks, except that mallards are reputed to mate for life. I wonder how that is related, if at all. I also notice that Mrs. Mallard has some sort of heart condition and her husband just died. If your spouse has just died, how do you think you would take the news?

Silvia: It would be shocking, you would think. But maybe it wasn't a good marriage. I mean like maybe the guy was abusive, so maybe she will be glad.

Mr. Victor: Then why would they "take great care to break" the news "as gently as possible"?

Alyssa: She has a heart condition, so the news could be shocking and cause her to have a heart attack.

Silvia: Yeah, even if the guy was like abusive, they were married and all, and hearing that he died could be a shock.

Mr. Victor: So, here is how the story continues: "It was her sister Josephine who told her, in broken sentences; veiled hints that revealed in half concealing. Her husband's friend Richards was there, too, near her. It was he who had been in the newspaper office when intelligence of the railroad disaster was received, with Brently Mallard's name leading the list of 'killed.' He had only taken the time to assure himself of its truth by a second telegram, and had hastened to forestall any less careful, less tender friend in bearing the sad message." I notice here that everyone is concerned about shocking Mrs. Mallard. In the first paragraph, the narrator tells us that Mrs. Mallard has a heart condition. Telling us early about the heart condition alerts me to pay special attention to this detail. I also note that Mr. Mallard died in a "railroad disaster." That sounds horrible to me. He must have died in a horrible, violent way. You can well imagine a collision or a derailment, with crunching metal, cracking timber, screaming passengers being hurled about train compartments. Of course, any sensitive spouse would find this news to be shocking and have a sense of empathy for the pain and horror her husband must have experienced. I would hope that if my wife heard the news of my sudden and unexpected death, she would find this distressing.

Silvia: You never know. It depends on the kind of marriage you have, or maybe your wife just wants to be on her own.

Mr. Victor: Well, I hope that isn't the case. I think it would be monstrous behavior to be anything but saddened by hearing about the violent death of a spouse. Now, I read through the first two paragraphs and shared my thinking as I moved along. I want you to do the same thing. In your groups, take turns, a couple of paragraphs at a time in reading aloud and thinking aloud. In the end, I want you to share with each other what you think about Mrs. Mallard's reaction to her husband's death.

The descriptions above illustrate a three-step sequence: discussing an image from popular culture to discover rules for notice and signification, applying rules to a constructed text, and practicing further with a more complex text. We advise that such a sequence would be appropriate for helping students to become aware of procedures for constructing meaning and evaluating a text. A teacher would not want to repeat this process several times. But if students were able to become aware of what to notice and how to apply meaning to the text features that they notice, they should be able to apply the same procedures in working with longer works, including *Animal Farm*, *Candide*, *Twelfth Night*, *Pride and Prejudice*, or *Cat's Cradle*. Of course, identifying the elements of a narrative that an author probably expected an audience to notice and sharing a rational basis for constructing meaning from these elements is just part of the process of interpreting and appraising a literary text. As demonstrated in the next chapter, readers will also want to be aware of the ways that longer narratives are structured.

YOUR VIEW

This chapter suggests that teachers need to do more than *assign* reading and then *assess* learners through recitation or quizzes. We encourage teachers to teach explicitly the procedures that mature readers rely on to interpret texts. The instructional process that we offer here moves from simple to complex and from teacher-initiated activities to more independent efforts. Most importantly, we want to engage learners in activities that will help them to become aware of procedures for actively working with texts, especially in imitation of what mature readers of literature typically do. Perhaps the steps we describe in this chapter seem too elementary for you and your students. If so, what alternative processes would you follow? Consider the following questions and discuss them with your colleagues.

1. If you judge that students should simply be assigned to read complex texts and grapple their way through the texts on their own, what benefits do you see from these experiences? If you doubt the efficacy of assigning reading without modeling or other preparation, what efforts do you see as appropriate for helping students to become aware of processes for constructing meaning?
2. If it makes sense to begin a multistage process by discussing images or films or other artifacts from popular culture, what texts, broadly defined, would you use? Why do you judge that these selections would be appealing to students and useful for achieving your learning targets?

Chapter 4

As Patterns Emerge

Joining along and Questioning Why

Reading research reveals that readers work with texts by following a process of progressive refinement (Collins, Brown, & Larkin, 1980) and use their conceptions of ideal story structure to organize their recall of what they have read (Mandler & Johnson, 1977). When students have an awareness of how writers commonly organize narratives, they can use this knowledge to follow the progress of the story or a play. The recognition of the narrative's configuration is also part of reader's pleasure in reading and helps a reader to think critically about a text.

On the simplest level, students use their awareness of story structures to follow along and recall what they have read. Viewers of movies on the Hallmark channel find enjoyment from the reassuring promise that the narrative will play out exactly as they expect and hope. Readers find the same satisfaction in reading a variety of genres that allow them to predict with confidence and have their expectations satisfied.

On another level, readers experience satisfaction and enjoyment in seeing how the author finds novel ways to reach the anticipated end. Readers note how a plot might have twists and turns and unexpected outcomes. These twists and turns can contribute to the delight that readers take in their reading. Viewers of the BBC's *Inspector Morse* or *Endeavor* series can expect that a murder has been committed and the inspector will identify and arrest the perpetrator by the end of the episode. The same is true for the old *Colombo* series. So, in a sense, the viewer knows what will happen before the episode begins. The pleasure for the viewer of the narrative is following the means toward the end: how the detective discovers how and why someone committed a murder. The process includes the tension between the perpetrator's attempts to distract and outwit the investigators and learning the detectives' procedures for solving the puzzle.

Similarly, the romance of the hero, or hero's journey, follows a predictable pattern. In fact, Joseph Campbell insists that there is but one hero's story told in perhaps thousands of variations. Recognizing the pattern and assuming the outcome does not spoil the fun in reading. One of the attractions for the reader is to experience an inventive variation in the episodic journey to the final confrontation with the villain.

By the time students have reached middle school, they have already experienced hundreds of narratives, in various media and genres. While the learners have this vast experience, they may never have reflected on the common patterns for narratives. An awareness of common ways that authors configure narratives can assist students in following along with the story, recalling what they have read, and reflecting critically on the implications of the work. The activities offered in this chapter should help learners to express their own set of *rules of configuration* (Rabinowitz, 1987) and apply these rules in working actively with a text to construct meaning.

RULES OF CONFIGURATION

When readers encounter a title like *The Tragedy of Hamlet, Prince of Denmark*, they know generally what is in store for the title character. The title invokes a mode of literature, suggests a predominantly grim view of human experience, and reveals that the outcome will be bad for Hamlet. Rabinowitz (1987) notes that "as we are reading, rules of configuration allow us to answer the question, 'How will this, in all probability work out?'" (112)

Rules of configuration are largely predictive. Some reading educators recommend teaching students the "strategy" of predicting, but the dynamic process of predicting, anticipating, re-evaluating, and reflecting is more complicated than a convenient strategy of guessing what's going to happen next. Readers rely on rules of configuration as they pass through a text and as they reflect on their reading: "Once we have finished the text, rules of configuration allow us to answer the question, 'How did this particular element make me think, at the time I encountered it, that the text would work out?'" (Rabinowitz, 1987, p. 112) Rabinowitz stresses this point: "A rule of configuration can be just as important to the reading experience when the outcomes it predicts turn out not to take place as when they do" (112).

In thinking about *rules of configuration*, think about three possibilities. First, the reader recognizes a pattern as it emerges: for example, two young people are attracted to each other, but narrow-minded elders stand in their way; a relatively inexperienced person is sent on a mission to suppress a threat to the community or to retrieve something that will benefit the community. As readers move through the text, they anticipate the episodes and complications, and they accurately predict an outcome.

Another possibility is that the elements that readers encounter early in a text suggest a predictable outcome, but the path to the outcome includes some unexpected and surprising variations on the conventional configuration. Again, this is perhaps part of the delight in reading some detective fiction, hero fantasies, and romantic comedies.

Yet another experience could be the author's intentional rupture of the usual configuration. This might be problematic for some readers, like expecting an attractive young couple to marry by the end of the play, only to have them kill themselves. Or, the rupture to the predictable pattern might suggest an ironic reading of the text, inviting readers to reflect on the implications of this reversal or to reflect on their own expectations for a desired outcome. Any of these variations—satisfaction, confrontation, irritation, puzzlement, or provocation—are part of the critical reading experience.

Consistent with the recommendations throughout this book, it would *not* be a good idea for the teacher to compile a list of *rules of configuration* and then project them for students and prod them to copy them down. Instead, with some effort to tap into what students already know, a teacher can facilitate discussions that can lead a class to construct their own rules of configuration. These might be different from the rules that Rabinowitz has noted or that we might devise, but the point is that students have an awareness of patterns of narratives and can use this awareness to help them to work with a text and reflect critically on its implications.

TAPPING INTO PRIOR KNOWLEDGE

The following sequence helps students to construct their own rules of configuration and then apply these rules when projecting how a narrative will develop or when reflecting on how the narrative developed compared to the way the reader anticipated. As a general instructional principle, a teacher will meet students where they are—tapping into knowledge from popular culture—and then moving to simple and then more complicated narratives. The activity below, "Paradise Cinema, Happy Anniversary," generates two levels of discussion (pairs and then whole class) and prompts students to construct their own rules of configuration.

PARADISE CINEMA: HAPPY ANNIVERSARY

The Paradise Cinema, a classic movie palace in Chicago, celebrated the 100th anniversary of its opening by holding a contest. The winner won a free pass for two for a year's worth of theater-going.

Here is the format for the contest: The staff of the Paradise Cinema drew from their archives the names and advertising copy for some of the more obscure movies shown at the theater during its early days. The challenge was for contestants to match the title of the movie with its synopsis. The films are so obscure that it is very difficult to find references to them through any search engines or histories of the cinema. Since there would likely be several correct submissions, the key factor in determining the winner was the *rationale* offered for making each match.

Let's try our hand at the contest. Even though the deadline for the original contest has passed, the winner from our class will receive an appropriate prize. *With a partner, complete the attached contest form.* Be prepared to explain to your classmates how you made your matches.

Movie Titles:

1. *Love Finds Bert Quimby*
2. *The Adventures of Beatrix Perez, the Pirate Queen*
3. *Sam Barnacle, Seaman*
4. *The Apprenticeship of Owen Betterbee*
5. *The Fall of Sarah Maudlin*
6. *Cat's Eye Mystery*
7. *Down These Dark Alleys*
8. *The Tragedy of Cameron Lauterdale*
9. *Bert Quimby Learns His Lessons*
10. *Sing Out for Love!*

Partners will examine the titles, which suggest specific narrative movements, and connect these projections with the descriptions. In the process, the students will offer a rationale for each match. If teachers do indeed treat the activity as a contest, students should submit one copy of the contest form, see (Table 4.1) before the students discuss their matches with the whole class. When the students explain their matches, the teacher can listen for statements that sound like rules and then record the rules for everyone to see. The following composite exchange represents a typical reporting of the students' matches, which includes the expression of rules of configuration.

Ms. Shannon: Let's hear from a team to see how you figured out your matches. How did you decide which descriptions fit with which titles?

Meera: So, we thought that letter A was *Bert Quimby Learns His Lessons*. The description says that the hero will teach the college professors, so that is the only one that says anything about school so we could eliminate the other ones and pick this one.

Table 4.1 Contest Form: Matching Titles and Stories

Synopsis	Match #	How did you know to make this match?
a. In this mad-cap romp, our beloved hero takes some of the starch out of college professors and turns the tide for the women's rowing team.		
b. The quest to find and return a stolen chalice to its rightful place requires a perilous journey and the ultimate confrontation with a murderous villain.		
c. When a young person enjoys a promotion at work and recognition in the community, life seems a happy idyll, until one bad decision brings hardship and regret.		
d. A young orphan, facing few options for survival, signs on as a cabin boy to the notorious Captain Hempstead on a voyage of danger and discovery.		
e. Several unexplained phenomena leave the town of Destiny Grove uneasy and throw suspicion on the reclusive tenant at the end of the lane.		
f. A young couple meet by chance at a community corn shucking event and are immediately attracted to each other, but the parents on both sides have been feuding for years. Through the use of disguise, the couple finds a way to meet outside of their parents' supervision, leading to awkward moments and an unexpected but satisfying end.		
g. Detective Beril Rigsby knows each sordid inch of the metropolis, but finding the perpetrator of a string of heinous crimes will require more than a map and a compass. Will Beril see through distractions to find the true culprit?		
h. The heir to an estate and a coveted title finds life descending into a hellish region of corruption and shame, brought on by greed and ambition.		
i. How does one bid farewell to the world of childhood and enter the adult world of travails and challenges? How does one find inner strength and kind assistance to pass through the many episodes of life and learn much about human nature?		
j. When Sally Linnet joined the Travelling Arts Theater Company, she dreamed only about being a small part of the magic of the theater, until an accident to the lead soprano and the encouragement of young Dane Sparrow thrust Sally center stage.		

Emmett: We agreed with that and thought that it was supposed to be funny, like the college freshman somehow teaching the professors like it is the opposite of the way it is supposed to be. And the guy is supposed to help the women's rowing team, maybe by being disguised as a woman or something. So, the guy on the women's rowing team is also the opposite. And the title made us think about a movie about a guy who learns sort of like "life lessons" when in college you are supposed to learn what you need for a career.

Ms. Shannon: OK, that makes some sense. The description suggested to you that there would be a reversal of the way things normally are, and the title suggested something funny, not seriously about learning lessons in a classroom. Does anyone have another match?

Lydia: We talked about letter H being *The Fall of Sarah Maudlin*. The description sounds like a person is in a pretty good position, like pretty well off and everything, and then something happens to cause the person to experience a lot of bad stuff.

Troy: Yeah, and the description says that the bad stuff happens because of her greed and ambition. So, she starts off well but does things herself to cause her to have trouble in the end.

Maddie: In our group, we kind of thought the same thing, but the movie *The Tragedy of Cameron Lauterdale* could match the description, too. We also thought that description C could fit either movie title.

Ms. Shannon: How do the two movies seem to be the same?

Maddie: For each one, the character is in a good place at the beginning but makes a bad decision or something and then gets into a lot of trouble. It sounds like each case ends in a bad place, like tragic.

Ms. Shannon: So, we could say that there are some movies or stories that feature a main character who starts of in a good position but makes some bad decisions or does something wrong to cause a downfall. That sounds like some sort of rule, like the rule of downfall following bad choices.

Cassandra: Yeah. Usually when you see someone in a really good place at the beginning of a movie, you know that something bad or complicated is going to happen to that character. I mean, it wouldn't be very interesting if the person is in a good place and everything goes well for the rest of the movie.

Lawrence: That would be boring.

RECOGNIZING RULES OF CONFIGURATION

A teacher can expect such a discussion to continue for some time, perhaps extending into a second class meeting. In facilitating the discussion, the teacher needs to be listening for statements that sound like rules. In the discussion above, two students notice something common among narratives: that the condition of a central character cannot remain static. If the narrative begins with a central character or characters in a good position, the fortunes of that character are likely to decline or at least get complicated. The arc of the narrative might be a further rise and then decline in fortune, as in tragedy, or a decline and then ascent, as in comedy.

During such discussions, students express rules that are specific to genres, like detective fiction or horror stories. When students compare the possibilities offered in the inquiry-based activity with their own experience as readers and viewers, they recognize patterns of narratives. Students can rely on this recognition or awareness to express "rules." You can find below an example of a set of rules that derive from class discussions. Students in your own classes are likely to express similar rules, in one form or another. It is not important that students use this exact language; it is important that they experience a *process* of recognizing patterns from their own reading and viewing and of giving some expression to what they have recognized.

DERIVED *RULES OF CONFIGURATION*

- Rule of attraction: Two young people seem destined to be a couple, but several obstacles, including their own misperceptions, stand in the way until all problems are resolved.
- Rule of reversal: Events of a narrative progress in a way that is the opposite of what "normally" occurs or the way that the central characters expect events to occur, prompting some uncomfortable humor and suggesting some cynicism.
- Rule of resolution: A problem baffles many characters, but one persistent thinker will not be misled and concludes what has occurred and explains the resolution to others.
- Rule of potential rise and then decline: A sympathetic character (i.e., one who elicits sympathy) advances in good fortune for a time but makes bad decisions that lead to a downfall in the end.
- Rule of journey and return: A central character completes an arduous journey in order to battle a daunting enemy and bring some benefit to a community.
- Rule of success: A humble character experiences a series of problems, failures, and accomplishments in order to achieve some stature in a given field of endeavor.

PRACTICE WITH RULES OF CONFIGURATION

We see the construction of a set of rules as a necessary step before proceeding to the application of the rules to involve readers in a story and project its resolution. Again, it is not important that students predict accurately; it is more important that readers draw from their knowledge of how narratives work in order to predict outcomes. In the end, for the sake of supporting the development of strong readers and foster an enthusiasm for reading, it is critical that students have a command of the procedures necessary for following a narrative, recalling what they read, and reflecting on the implications. A command of the procedures comes with practice.

The following activity with a narrative helps students to talk about their awareness of patterns and to offer a logical basis for their predictions. The sample dialogue below comes from preservice teachers in a university teacher preparation program, but middle school and high school students will respond in a similar but less elaborated way. The story comes from Nora O'Flynn and is reproduced here by permission and generosity of the O'Flynn family of Manchester, England.

The following directions prepare students for reading and discussing a brief, incomplete narrative. The full narrative appears as an appendix to this book. Following the directions, students should work in three stages: (1) decide independently what will happen to Alfred, (2) discuss conjectures with partners in a small group, and (3) share across a class the predictions that teams offered and explore how the knowledge of rules of configuration might have directed the predictions. It is also useful to engage students in an online discussion of their predictions and the bases for the predictions.

WHAT WILL HAPPEN TO ALFRED?

Directions: The title of the story reveals in part what must happen in the story "Poor Alfred, Buried Three Times." Based on what you know about how narratives are constructed, what do project as the resolution of the story? What "rules" guide your projection?

POOR ALFRED, BURIED THREE TIMES

Nora O'Flynn

On the beach at the east end of Clare Island, County Mayo, Ireland, a body washed ashore. Children at play discovered the body, blue in the exposed flesh, entangled by seaweed, repeatedly washed by the rhythmic surf. The children screamed and ran to find adults to remove the corpse from the place of their accustomed play.

The year was 1925. The English still dominated the Irish and held most civil service posts, including those on Clare Island. There were two college-educated residents on the island—Father McNamara, pastor of the Church of the Sacred Heart, and Mr. McGreal, headmaster at Saint Patrick National School. Once every month, Father McNamara was allowed to leave the island and visit the mainland of Ireland. In his absence, Mr. McGreal was consulted for advice and enlisted for quasi-ecclesiastical duties. Such was the case on this August morning.

Tim O'Malley, a fisherman, and Pat Burns, a farmer, having covered the corpse and loaded it on Pat's cart, went to the home of Mr. McGreal to seek advice about the disposal of the body. The three consulted in the front yard of the McGreal home and decided without question that the body must be buried immediately. No one could properly identify the disfigured body of the man who had died. There seemed no sign of foul play, and a death by drowning was common in the frigid waters of Clew Bay. Since there was no morgue on the island and no means of refrigeration to preserve the body, the three men recognized a keen sense of decency and a need for proper sanitation that the body must be interred as soon as possible.

Mr. McGreal collected his prayer book and a spade and headed to the churchyard adjacent to the ruins of a Cistercian abbey. Tim O'Malley ran to Cleary's Pub near the quay to recruit mourners for this impromptu funeral. On the way, he called to farmers in their fields to urge them to bring a shovel and meet at the churchyard. After all assembled and the grave was dug, the corpse of the drowned man, wrapped in a tarp from Tim O'Malley's boat, was lowered into the grave. Mr. McGreal opened his prayer book and said an appropriate prayer for the dead. The few in attendance lowered their heads solemnly and mumbled a Hail Mary.

By the time Father McNamara returned to the island the next day, word of the drowned man had reached many residents on the island, and it was discovered that the man was likely Alfred Kitchums, the lighthouse keeper who had gone missing for several days. Men at Cleary's Pub discussed the matter soberly until Fergus Gavan noted that Alfred, a government-employed lighthouse keeper, was Anglo-Irish and most certainly a Protestant. And, noted Fergus, shaking his head gravely, was this not a sacrilege for Mr. McGreal and his accomplices to bury Alfred Kitchums, a known Protestant, in the consecrated ground of a Roman Catholic cemetery? The men wisely concluded that something must be done to correct this desecration as soon as possible.

At a decent hour the next morning, the men from Cleary's Pub called on Father McNamara, who had returned to the island, to share their conclusions and to recommend action to exhume the offending body from the consecrated ground. Father McNamara judged it most appropriate to call on Mr. McGreal to hear his side of the story. Mr. McGreal invited the small party into his home for tea, over which they agreed that the unacceptable deposit of Alfred in the Catholic cemetery was a more honest mistake than conscious sacrilege, but they still needed to know what to do to correct matters.

Fergus Gavan offered that there might be some profit in consulting with Tim O'Malley and Pat Burns, whom he suspected were standing at the bar in Cleary's Pub by now. So the men removed to the pub, where they found Tim and Pat standing at the bar, leaning over their pints. After a quick review of the facts and the shaking of heads all around, the men were at a loss for a solution. There was only one cemetery on the island, and decency and safety called for the body to remain buried; yet sacrilege threatened the spiritual welfare and compromised the moral standing of all involved. After a bit of whisky and a second pint, Pat Burns offered generously to allow Alfred to be buried at the back of his potato field. He recalled that there was a small plot of ground that he allowed to go fallow each year, and he would have no difficulty with a Protestant taking up eternal residence near his potato crop. All the men saw the wisdom and generosity in this offer.

So, the next morning, the assembled men dug up the remains of Alfred from the churchyard near the abbey and solemnly carted him to the back of Pat Burns' potato field. There, before the prepared grave, Father McNamara said prayers for the dead and reminded all the men that death could visit them at any time, just as it had unexpectedly visited Alfred, and that they must be prepared to face judgment at any moment of their lives. They all recited a Hail Mary and crossed themselves.

The following spring, after the word of Alfred's death had reached many of Alfred's relatives and friends on the mainland of Ireland and in England, they began to appear on Clare Island, sometimes unloading from the ferry in small groups. The friendly residents pointed the way to Pat Burns' farm and described where to find the gravesite. It did not take many such visits for Pat to discover that the relatives and friends cut across his field, trampling the spreading potato rills and threatening his crop. Initially, he had been happy to accommodate the unfortunate Alfred, but he could not allow his crop to be ruined by these many visitors. Pat invited Father McNamara, Mister McGreal, and all interested parties on the island to meet at Cleary's Pub to seek a solution to the current dilemma.

DISCUSSING THE STORY

The following exchange comes from an extended online discussion about the story "Poor Alfred, Buried Three Times." Seventeen class members contributed to the discussion, and only a few excerpts appear here. The references to the class's derived rules of configuration appear in italics.

Haylie: Based on what we have read so far in this story, and the *sense of irony* that is occurring, I believe that Alfred's final burial will, in following the irony, be at sea, where he started. None of the men can seem to come up with the right place to bury Alfred, in considering the values he likely held before death, and, as the story progresses, it seems as though they are all becoming more plagued by this body, and they want to find one last and appropriate resting place not only for Alfred but also for themselves, in order to rid themselves of what has now become somewhat of a burden.

Therefore, it seems likely, and in line with the ironic ideologies that the men presented before, to lay Alfred to rest at sea, where he was initially found. In doing so, the men will be laying Alfred to rest in a place that is familiar to him as a lighthouse keeper, while also getting him out of their hair and ensuring that he is no longer a burden on their physical spaces. This could also serve as another point of irony, then, as the men believe that they are physically getting rid of Alfred and his burden for good, though it seems likely that Alfred and all of these events will continue to burden their thoughts and minds, based on the emotions and reactions they have displayed so far.

Poor Alfred, and the irony of it all—being buried and dug up twice, only to end up where he started! However, while this chain of events that I created may seem fruitless for the men involved, I believe that all of it did serve a purpose in reminding the men that death is present and inescapable. At Alfred's second burial, Father McNamara "reminded all the men that death could visit them at any time, just as it had unexpectedly visited Alfred, and that they must be prepared to face judgment at any moment of their lives." Therefore, while there is the irony that Alfred ended up back in the cemetery where he started, thus rendering the efforts of the men useless, these events still served as a lesson for the men in considering that death could come upon them at any time, and, as such, they should live their lives well and hope that, when their time comes, they will be treated with respect in death—something that they tried to do with Alfred, but did not achieve.

Jessica: My first suspicion that this story is going to go awry is the description of the body "was *likely* Alfred Kitchums" (my italics). There is no moment in the text that tells the reader that the body is, without a doubt, that of Alfred. Maybe the lighthouse was in a remote location? Maybe Alfred was a bit of a recluse? Maybe his relatives hated him and so wanted to see the spot where he was buried to make sure he was truly dead? The role of lighthouse keeper is a lonely one, and it is quite possible the "real" Alfred is still alive and it is merely a macabre game of "telephone" that we are falling prey to, along with Alfred's family.

I can't help but think of the fierce animosity between Catholics and Protestants in Ireland at this time (thank you, Joyce) and I suppose my first instinct is to be touched that the men who buried "Alfred" the first (second?) time were concerned about his religion enough to exhume the body and rebury it. Or, they really just wanted the Protestant body out of their Catholic churchyard, citing religious bias and a baseness of character that is exemplified through this act as they scramble to save their own souls. Either way, the tension that is added through the competing religions is complete when the men say a "Hail Mary" at a Protestant burial on unconsecrated ground. Truly, it's insulting.

As we are dealing with a case of possible mistaken identity, I would like to see a *Rule of Success* occur wherein Alfred triumphantly returns from his lonely sojourn at the lighthouse to be mistaken for an (ironically) Catholic saint or something of the sort and is hailed as a kind of hero and lives the rest of his life with no shortage of potatoes and pints.

Keaton: If we assume the title to be factual with how the story will end up then we know that Alfred will be buried one more time, but we don't know how. We are told that many of Alfred's relatives and friends are coming from the mainland to pay their respects so perhaps Alfred could return to the mainland with them and be buried there. Or, as others have pointed out, Alfred may be laid to rest near his lighthouse if he must be interred on the island as it is a place of significance for him and, although not beholding to his religious views, would likely be a resting place that would please Alfred.

Something else that might be considered is that, since the title says "buried three times," maybe Alfred is moved yet again but, this time, is not buried at all. Others have already mentioned that putting Alfred to rest at sea might be fitting for the character and that would resolve any and all issues of finding a suitable plot.

Another key detail is that the story states that "the man was LIKELY Alfred Kitchums," which implies that maybe the man was someone else entirely. Yes, Alfred had been missing for several days but perhaps he had simply taken a trip to the mainland, which we know is possible as there is a ferry to do so and potential motive, as maybe he was visiting relatives at the time.

Also, the body was found in the water so, whoever it was, was not guaranteed to have died on the island and could have possibly been simply washed there from another region. It is entirely possible that the story could end with the body being buried at a settled upon location only for the real Alfred to show up and ask what all the fuss is about.

Simply put, the only firm indicator we have about how the story progresses/ends is the title. And that only tells us that "Alfred" is buried one more time. After taking that fact into account, all other interpretations are based on snippets of information that we have been given, which may or may not be altered by the continuation of the story. The evidence about "Alfred" himself can clue us into how he may end up (that he worked the lighthouse, that he had relatives on the mainland, that he was a Protestant, etc.) and we can attempt to formulate an ending from there. However, there is always the possibility of a twist ending which, by its very nature, would be unpredictable even with all our current evidence.

Allison: The men in the town have been trying to do right by Alfred's remains, so I believe they will try and come up with a more appropriate place to bury him. Now that his family is in town, they may be able to offer some advice about what Alfred had wanted for his remains. Perhaps the family will take him home and bury him, or perhaps they will bury him on more private land so that his family and friends can come and visit him without disturbing anyone's land. From the title of the story, we know that this burial of Alfred will be the last, so I am hopeful that they will find an appropriate place for his remains. Adding a twist to the story, one could say that Pat Burns, who was gracious enough to lend his land, is now going to suffer at the hands of Alfred's ghost after having his body moved again.

The little bit I added about Tim comes from the *rule of potential rise and decline*. He will gain sympathy from the people in the town for allowing Alfred to be buried at the expense of his field and will gain some success from it. But, after having Alfred's body moved, he will meet his downfall in the end.

From the rules we have derived, I would say that the *rule of resolution* has guided my answer. Pat Burns has been involved since the beginning in trying to determine what will become of Alfred, and despite a misstep with placing Alfred in the potato field, I think he wants nothing more than to do right by him, so he will be the leader when it comes to determining what to do with Alfred.

Additionally, I think the *rule of reversal* has also come into play, as some people would say the story should have started with identifying the body and coming up with a proper burial plan rather than unearthing the remains several times. The uncomfortable humor is that the men want to bury Alfred, but they have absolutely no approach to what they are doing; they are simply doing what they think may be considered right.

Danielle: I think the title of the story sets our expectations that Alfred (if it is, in fact, Alfred's body that's been found) will be disinterred yet again and buried for a third time. Although the title of the story does give us some ideas about its likely ending, I do think it's also misleading to the extent that the title implies the story is actually one focused on a character named Alfred. I rather think it becomes a commentary on how indifference and self-interest can very quickly lead to something as seemingly absurd as burying and re-burying a poor deceased person's body three times.

I think the rule that essentially helped me arrive at this ending and interpretation is the *rule of reversal*. While I do not think that Alfred is particularly sympathetic in the traditional sense, I do think that his assumed corpse is treated in ways that run in direct opposition to the manner in which we would expect a small, close-knit, caring community would care for the remains and process the loss of one of their own.

FURTHER PRACTICE

The exchange reproduced above is an example of students working together to apply their derived rules in anticipating the outcome for the narrative. The entries in the discussion reveal that the students recalled much of the narrative, which is basic, and they call on rules of notice, rules of signification, and rules of configuration to anticipate an outcome. Students appear to take pleasure in the process of anticipating an outcome and reflecting on their bases for conjectures. One student, Brian, reported: "This was fun. I really do wonder how the story actually ended. Please let us know soon. I'm anxious to find that he gets a better coffin than a tarp."

But this was a simple narrative. The obvious next instructional steps are to practice again and again with more complex texts and with a variety of narratives and dramas. Perhaps a class could get into the routine of reading the beginning of narratives slowly and carefully to anticipate where the narrative will take them. Such a routine is likely to prepare students for reading and foster some enthusiasm for the task.

YOUR VIEW

By the time you encounter students in middle school or high school, they will have experienced at least hundreds of narratives—by reading, viewing, or listening. Their experience with stories includes their immersion into the narratives that provide the structures for video games. You and your colleagues might discuss how you can tap into students' considerable experience with narratives to help them to become aware of patterns and use this awareness to drive their reading and to reflect on the meaning they construct from it.

1. How can you design experiences to tap into students' prior knowledge to construct rules of configuration rather than trying to transmit a prepared list of rules?

2. If you judge that different cultures have distinctly different ways for structuring stories and for expecting narratives to develop, how are these ways distinct, and how can you honor the distinctions to help students to draw from their knowledge to help them recall their reading and reflect on a text's implications?

Chapter 5

Introducing Competing Critical Views

Imagine a group of friends leaving an "art" movie theater and gathering for coffee after their viewing together of a film. The friends are eager to talk about the film, an adaptation of Mary McCarthy's *The Group*; but they all have walked away with different impressions.

Bonnie: I think the director really didn't like women.
Kristen: Why do you say that?
Bonnie: Every one of the female characters is flawed: neurotic, dishonest, promiscuous, needy.
Bob: And all of the men were depicted as ignorant, cold-hearted fiends. There wasn't any man who was at all sensitive or compassionate. Maybe the bipolar father, but he seemed oblivious to the effects of the demands he was imposing on his daughter.
Bonnie: And the one strong, confident, and admired member of the group was a lesbian, and she kind of gets shipped off to Europe at the opening of the film, as soon as the women graduate from Vassar. I don't know if that meant a kind of ostracism or McCarthy was implying that Lakey had to go to Europe to escape puritanical ideas in the United States.
Richard: I did notice that the only Black actor in the film was a maid serving punch at a party. Much of the story takes place in Manhattan, yet there are no Black characters, except in a generic role, without even a line of dialogue, if I recall.
Kristen: I suppose that was a product of the time. The movie was from 1966, and the novel was earlier. I guess that casting directors and film directors were less inclusive at that time. And McCarthy was probably drawing from the circle of social elite that she knew.

Richard: That's interesting—what Bonnie was saying about Lakey. The friends encourage her to return from Europe because World War II was brewing. There is this kind of major political turmoil in Europe, but the film deals with it just around the edges. I mean, there are characters, like the publisher, the Hal Holbrook character, who refer to political ideas the way you would talk about the latest fad diet or exercise regime. He says he goes to meetings of the communist party, but he has not actually a "card-carrying" communist. It is as if he was going to a Rotary Club meeting or something. What's the point of simply referring to communism or fascism? Did McCarthy want to say anything about either one? That fascism was really bad and that communism wasn't as bad as people thought?

Kristen: In fact, he doesn't seem committed to anything. He uses the lame excuse that he had promised his wife to complete therapy before they divorce. He is not committed to marriage, but he is not firm about a divorce.

Bonnie: I hadn't really thought about the political part. I saw that as the historical background for the women. Their day-to-day lives had enough challenges without worrying about fascism and communism in Europe. I was concerned about how the women would survive in their relationship. It was like Richard saw a whole different movie.

Perhaps you have participated in such conversations. Sometimes they can be frustrating, especially when one person dominates the conversation and assumes a position of authority. But such conversations are often rather satisfying. One reason that the talk about the experience with the film can be satisfying is that the discussants are all contributing impressions or insights that expand everyone's thinking about the film. In the brief exchange above, someone offers a gendered angle, someone discusses possible political implications, someone recalls the historical backdrop for the novel and the film and the possible personal interests of the author. These are just a few views expressed in a brief exchange. In a longer conversation, over several cups of coffee, the views could expand and open up new possibilities for viewing and judging the film, even to the point where, as Bonnie says above, it seems that each friend had experienced a different film.

The reality is that all viewers of a film or readers of a narrative will have distinct experiences. There is likely to be some common understandings across a group, but inevitably everyone's view will be at least slightly different. This is because all readers will bring different knowledge, interests, and predispositions to the experience. When someone says, "It seems that you watched an entirely different film," the comment could imply that, in a sense, someone else did not actually experience the film at all or experienced it only shallowly or narrowly.

The impression that one had an entirely different viewing or reading experience suggests that readers of a novel or a play typically miss much on first reading or without engaging with others in rich conversations about what they have read. There clearly are benefits to being exposed to a variety of views or a context, even if some views challenge your assumptions or contrast with what you judge to be carefully wrought interpretations and discerning judgments. When we bump into views that challenge our own, we have an opportunity to reflect on our own conclusions and check that our analysis and evaluation are grounded in logic and not drawn merely from quick impressions driven by our own biases. Even when another reader largely agrees with you, you might find that the other thinker exposes some previously missed possibilities or offers a more persuasive or nuanced analysis.

As Graff (2008; 2009) points out, there isn't much to discuss or write about unless we are aware of disagreements or areas of doubt. After all, who would want to read an argument about an interpretation that seems to be universally embraced or an assessment that is widely shared? A dissertation writer will review the literature related to the focus of the report. This is not a cruel task imposed to initiate the novice scholar into the field of research. Instead, the review helps the writer to frame a problem and to show where the new research fits into the broader conversation in the field of inquiry. In a more modest way, high school students and university students can become aware of possibilities for reading and judging a text so that in representing these possibilities, they can demonstrate the significance or relevance to what they have to say.

This chapter does not suggest ways to introduce students to complex philosophical stances or highly technical ways for reading and discussing literature. Instead, there are relatively simple ways by which a teacher can invite students to look at a work of literature through a variety of critical lenses and to learn how to engage productively with others in talking about the merits of various critical possibilities. As a general instructional principle, it makes sense to begin simply and then move to increasingly more complex concepts or procedures, to move from instruction that is highly dependent on the teacher to the students' more independent efforts. The following sequence of activities illustrates ways to invite learners to look at complex works through various critical lenses and to give students opportunities to practice the procedures that Graff notes as "academic intellectual discourse" (Graff, 2003).

INTERROGATING DR. SEUSS AND OTHER AUTHORS

An earlier book (McCann & Knapp, 2021) offers some relatively simple ways to encourage students to look at texts from several critical perspectives. Appleman (2014/2000) offers other possibilities and provides more technical explorations for selected critical lenses. As the dialogue above illustrates, everyone will likely experience a text through a unique personal lens, but a teacher can expand possibilities and perhaps exaggerate differences by introducing lenses that have a fairly long critical tradition.

Specifically, many students might find it awakening and provoking to consider a text from a historical/biographical, gendered, psychological, or political perspective. This is not to say that high school students need to be aware of academic arguments for the legitimacy or necessity of reading a text through any one of these lenses. *Still*, as Smith, Wilhelm, and Appleman (2014) note, the dominant critical approach to reading and discussing literature in schools has been some form of New Criticism; moreover, with the imposition of the Common Core State Standards and guidance offered by their main advocate (Coleman, 2011), the pervasive approach could be termed a kind of "Zombie New Criticism," as other have noted.

The obvious limitation to the approach is that readers are supposed to restrict themselves to the features of the text, with little regard for the influences of history and politics, knowledge about human psychology, or concerns about issues of equity and justice. Graff (1992; 2003) encourages injecting conflict into classroom conversations about literature and offers guidance for navigating the discourse moves when constructing meaning in the midst of doubt and disagreement (Graff, G., Birkenstein, C. & Durst, 2018).

Putting students in a situation in which they have to contend with multiple possibilities for interpreting and evaluating a text invites their entry into intellectual academic discourse. This does not mean that they need to imitate the way scholars talk about the text in a very technical and perhaps esoteric way. Graff (2003) speaks of his own student days where friends parodied their teachers at parties, but "strained for the very preciosity we had satirized the night before" during the next days in class (p. 126). Learning academic discourse does mean that learners have to pay attention to the ideas of others, represent those ideas fairly, and evaluate those possibilities as they advance their own analyses and conclusions.

As we suggest in our earlier chapters, a common instructional sequence moves students from relatively simple concepts and procedures to increasingly complex concepts and procedures. The sequence would also move students from much initial reliance on the teacher to more independent effort. The following chart (figure 5.1) suggests such a sequence, which the balance of this chapter illustrates.

INTRODUCING CRITICAL LENSES: WHAT HAPPENED ON MULBERRY STREET?

High school students are often reluctant to debate each other about conflicting interpretations of a work of literature. They are also hesitant to entertain various and conflicting interpretations of a text. A common criticism is that

Introducing Competing Critical Views

```
┌─────────────────────────────────────────┐
│ Introduce the concept of looking at a   │
│ text through various critical lenses    │
├─────────────────────────────────────────┤
│ Texts: children's story, image or film  │
│ clip from popular culture, simple text  │
│ from popular culture                    │
└─────────────────────────────────────────┘
                    ⇩
┌─────────────────────────────────────────┐
│ Practice with using various critical    │
│ lenses for discussing a short narrative │
├─────────────────────────────────────────┤
│ Text: a short story that invites a      │
│ variety of critical views               │
└─────────────────────────────────────────┘
                    ⇩
┌─────────────────────────────────────────┐
│ Apply competing critical views to a     │
│ longer and more complex work of         │
│ literature                              │
├─────────────────────────────────────────┤
│ Texts: novellas, novels, plays, films   │
└─────────────────────────────────────────┘
```

Figure 5.1 A Sequence to Introduce and Practice with Critical Lenses. *Source*: Author created.

the teacher or some other eager reader in the class is "over analyzing" and ruining a good story by "taking it apart" and examining it "too deeply." The following activity prompts students to read a text from particular perspectives while also listening to and experiencing the organized viewpoints of a few other perspectives.

There are four perspectives represented in the prompts below. The four prompts would be distributed among an entire class, with each student receiving a single prompt. The assumption here is that the prompt will activate schema and influence students to consider a variety of interpretations that they will be capable of defending during classroom interchanges. Here is the procedure:

(1) Each student receives an envelope. The student's name and the number of the prompt are printed on the outside of the envelope. The students are encouraged to record and recall the number that appears on the outside of the envelope. In the envelope is a prompt (see the specific prompts below). The teacher instructs the students to read the

prompts silently. The teacher cautions the students not to share the "secret" prompt with anyone. The idea here is to encourage a variety of views to invite students into negotiation with their peers about how to read and evaluate the text. After reading the prompt, each student writes a brief response: *Do you agree with the ideas expressed in the envelope? Why? Do you disagree with the ideas? Why?* The students then place their written responses and the prompt back in the envelope and return the envelope to the teacher.

(2) The teacher then reads aloud Dr. Seuss's *And to Think That I Saw It on Mulberry Street*. (Note: An early version of the 1936 book would be most provocative.) As the teacher reads, she pauses occasionally to display the illustrations.

(3) After reading the story aloud, the teacher distributes a copy of the story to all the students (the text without the illustrations is available online). The teacher directs the students to read the story again silently.

(4) After the students have read the story, the teacher instructs them to write an explanation of the meaning of the story: "It is customary for the writers of children's stories to use the narrative and the accompanying illustrations to teach children a lesson. In this case, what lesson or message do you get from reading the story?"

(5) After the students have produced their written responses, they arrange their desks into a large circle. The students, however, will sit close to others who have read the same prompt: that is, all the *ones* are near each other, all of the *twos* are near each other, etc.

(6) The teacher selects someone at random to begin the discussion: "What do you think are the meanings of the story? What message(s) did you get from your reading?"

(7) Each subsequent speaker can continue only after he or she has paraphrased the response of the previous speaker. The idea here is to listen actively and to practice representing someone else's view.

(8) An observer will take notes: Record the comments of each speaker and note which prompt he or she received.

(9) Analyze the notes. Do students express multiple interpretations? Do they appropriately defend their own reading of the text? Are the students willing to challenge and respond to each other?

(10) After the discussion, the students will return to their initial written response to the story and then extend their writing by responding to the following questions: *Would you change anything? Do any of the other interpretations that you heard have any merit? Why, or why not? How have you been influenced by the discussion?*

Here are the four prompts to *prepare* for the reading of the text:

1. Delusions are dangerous. Each person must guard against imagining things that do not *really* exist. Of course, we all have dreams and fantasies, but we need to separate fantasy from reality. A person should not live in a dream world. Someone would clearly jeopardize his or her physical and emotional well-being by imagining and acting upon things that were not really there. It is likely that a habitual dreamer would alienate (i.e., turn away) other persons who are bound to think the dreamer is crazy.
2. Children have vivid imaginations that support their creativity and mental health. When children are very young, they can imagine unusual places, people, and circumstances. Look at a child's drawings sometime. They are very comfortable in drawing an orange sky and a purple cow. This does not mean that they have vision problems or that they are crazy. As each person grows older, he or she loses some of that ability to imagine, until we reach the point of focusing only on practical, dull, everyday concerns. Some writers and artists appreciate that parents need to encourage children in developing their imaginations.
3. An important function for parents is to keep their children firmly grounded in reality. For example, when a child sees a cartoon character fall from a cliff and get up to walk away, the child must realize that this cannot really happen. It would be dangerous for children to think that persons could *really* fly like Superman. A parent has a responsibility to help a child to make the distinction between fantasy and reality. A *limited* amount of dreaming might be harmless, but when the dreaming becomes exaggerated, a parent *must* intervene to make the child realize the reality of a situation.
4. Parents are often at fault for suppressing their children's imaginations. It is healthy for young children to engage in dreaming and imagining. Their fantasies provide a means for them to make sense of the world. Children use fantasies to express their hopes and their fears. Parents often lack sensitivity to those needs. Adults often discourage a child's imaginings because the adult must focus on the drudgery of everyday concerns. It is neither fair nor healthy for adults to judge children by adult standards.

OBJECTION TO READING A DR. SEUSS TEXT

Perhaps the pre-reading prompts and reflections position students to read the simple story in distinct ways, and the students find themselves engaged in a dialogic process with peers to evaluate possibilities, voice agreement or disagreement, and defend their own reading of the text. That would be the goal: to immerse learners in procedures for recognizing and evaluating alternative views and expressing a personal view and showing where that view fits into the critical conversation. But, consistent with the practices promoted by Graff (1992; 2003; 2009), a teacher can elevate the significance of the conversation by exposing students to some critical views that show Seuss under attack.

As of the writing of this book, several of Dr. Seuss's books for children have come under increased scrutiny, and some defenders dismiss criticism as the latest example of "cancel culture" (Chappell, 2021; Alter & Harris, 2021). There are at least three benefits to using the Dr. Seuss book to invite students to consider a work of literature through several critical lenses. One benefit is that there is an existing conflict and not an invented controversy. An obvious benefit is that the work is short and a teacher can guarantee that everyone in class will have read the text under discussion.

The third benefit is that the students can connect one text to several other texts by the same author. This is a rare experience in high school, or even at the university, outside of seminars that focus on the several works of a single author. In being able to connect one text to several others, students can speak to recurring themes and note consistencies or inconsistencies across a body of work.

After the initial and probably placid conversation about how to read the Dr. Seuss text, a teacher can share the following letter, asking students to imagine the teacher received such a strong letter of complaint. *How should the teacher respond? To what extent are the criticisms merited?*

Letter of Complaint about Dr. Seuss

Dear Teacher:

I strongly object to your reading of Dr. Seuss's *And to Think I Saw It on Mulberry Street*. Although the text appears at first glance to be a simple and innocent nonsense book for children, a close examination will reveal it to be sexist, racist, and generally destructive.

First of all, the book promotes the idea that women are unaccomplished and unworthy of positions of leadership. This implication is apparent in many ways. There are *no* female characters in the book. Apparently no women are worthy of a place in the world of Mulberry Street. The central character, Marco, is male. He hopes to impress and appease his *father,* and there is no mention of his mother, as if her opinion were worth nothing, or Marco came into the world without the efforts or contributions of a mother. When Marco ponders the products of his imagination, he dismisses a relatively simple image, because "even Jane could think of that." Obviously, Marco and Seuss see women as humans who suffer from arrested imagination.

As the parade of Mulberry dignitaries and luminaries increases, the reader notices that the mayor, the chief of police, the police officers, the fire department, musicians, pilots—indeed, all the leaders and gifted talents of Marco's world—are men. The vision offers several disturbing implications: that women are not capable enough to hold positions of power and leadership, that women are not to be entrusted with the protection of citizens and property, that women are not talented or skillful enough for roles that require judgment, dexterity, and physical strength. It is not sufficient to say that Seuss was a product of his time and was simply reporting the state of the world as it was in the 1930s. In the 1930s, as at other times throughout human history, there were many women who were leaders, artists, entrepreneurs, scholars, and scientists. Surely Seuss was familiar with important women such as Eleanor Roosevelt, Amelia Earhart, Mary Cassatt, Willa Cather, and Madame Curie. It was not a matter that he could see no examples of female leaders, artists, and scholars; he *chose* to ignore them as examples and role models.

Just as disturbing to the reader is Seuss's negative stereotyping of Asians and the elderly. In the original version of the text, Seuss refers to a "Chinaman with sticks." The illustration of this Asian character shows a comic figure with a long cue, a face distinctly yellow in complexion, and wearing platform slippers. He wears a cone-shaped bamboo hat and carries a bowl and chopsticks. What is the young reader to think? The implication is that Asian people are all alike, in physical appearance, and in their inclination to eat rice with wooden sticks. A caricature is an object of ridicule. Seuss is not even accurate. He portrays a Chinese character wearing the type of footwear that would be more like the kind of footwear worn in Japan, as if all Asians and all Asian culture were interchangeable. Furthermore, Seuss offers a "Rajah" as a representative of the subcontinent of Asia. At one time, a *rajah* would be a prince or ruler in India. The rajah is a person of high rank and prestige. To Seuss, however, he becomes a ridiculous figure in pajama-like attire and jeweled turban. Again, impressionable children are left with the misguided notion that citizens of India and their leaders are comic figures.

Perhaps my advanced age makes me hypersensitive to the next issue, but I must take exception to Dr. Seuss's portrayal of the elderly. One older character in the book is a man with flowing beard that "needs a comb." The other elderly gentleman also sports a long beard and sits idle on a stool on his front porch. It is difficult enough to influence young people to respect older adults; now Seuss sends the clear message that older persons are all bearded, slovenly, and inactive.

We might tolerate Seuss's errors if on balance his book sponsored a positive message, but it doesn't. Marco lets his imagination run free; but when he faces his father, he denies that he had any vision at all. The implication is that parents constrain and suppress their children. Clearly, Marco is intimidated by a father who hopes to condition him to be just as rigid, dull, and unimaginative as he. The author, perhaps unwittingly, promotes animosity between the youthful readers and their parents.

Sincerely,

N. S. Eastwhist

RESPONDING TO THE CRITIC

As you can imagine, many students have strong reactions to an attack on a work by Dr. Seuss and the expressed or implied attack on Dr. Seuss himself. Some students will point to the date of publication and excuse Dr. Seuss as simply representing the world and attitudes he saw around him, noting that in reality positions of power and leadership were dominated by men. Similarly, they will excuse the author for the ethnic stereotyping because he probably had limited experience with people from Asia. Others who recall several Seuss tales from their early childhood will insist that he is someone who actually combated prejudice with such stories as "The Sneeches."

In facilitating such a critical exchange, the teacher would want to paraphrase what each contributor has offered or insist that each speaker begins by paraphrasing the essential assessment from the previous speaker. Such a practice or protocol models how discussion participants can listen actively. The practice also helps everyone to follow the discussion because the speaker provides the context for the current contribution. In academic intellectual discourse, speakers or writers are able to represent the various views in an ongoing conversation and are able to show how their own remarks or analyses fit into and contribute to the conversation.

It is not an exaggeration to say that the examination of a simple text through competing critical lenses allows readers to experience the text again for the first time. It is not uncommon for readers to read *And to Think I Saw It on Mulberry Street* and note that they had never before been sensitive to some of the questionable images and the unfortunate implications. It would be fair for a reader to say, "I feel like I had never read the book at all."

EXTENDING PRACTICE WITH A SHORT NARRATIVE

Consider Shirley Jackson's often anthologized short story, "The Lottery." High school students are often required to read this story, and even middle-school students are sometimes asked to read it. It is a puzzling tale, inviting discussion to work through our puzzlement. Since the story was first published in 1948, it has triggered strong reactions, even outrage. The fact that there is a history of doubt about the story makes it perfect for examining through several critical lenses. While some anthology editors and a few teachers might want to reduce the story to a "theme" in the sense of a succinct axiom, the story defies easy interpretation, and perhaps we search in vain for some conventional theme. But the clash of critical views supports the value of our myriad attempts to understand and appreciate the story.

A teacher might want to introduce the reading of the text by noting that there is a long history of disagreement about how to interpret and judge the text. In fact, several readers canceled their subscription to *The New Yorker* after the story was first published, and *even* Jackson's own parents expressed disapproval of the work. What, if anything, is so disagreeable about the story?

After the students have read the story, one way to encourage the reexamination of the tale through various critical lenses is to assign students to small groups and ask each group to evaluate the extent to which a specific critical view seems to be a reasonable response to the story. A set of possible critical views appear below (figure 5.3).

Presuming that students have read the story, form seven groups, provide each group with a distinct critical view and offer these directions: In your group, read the critical view of the story. Prepare to explain this view for the rest of the class and evaluate the degree to which you judge that the view is a valid way to read the story. Keep in mind what you think the author expected us to notice and how you know that the elements you notice carry any significance.

Seven Critical Views of Shirley Jackson's "The Lottery"

a. *Someone must pay a price.* Shirley Jackson suggests that the occupants of the rural town have a vague notion that performing the lottery every year is a key to their prosperity. In fact, Old Man Warner, who serves to recall the traditions, notes, "Lottery in June, corn be heavy soon." Even if the residents don't understand the logical linkage between the lottery and their crop yields, they believe in the connection so strongly that they would not dare to abandon the lottery. Jackson, who grew up during the Great Depression, would recognize that in a free market economy, there will inevitably be winners and losers. Wealth is not distributed equally, but some portion of the population must be sacrificed, both economically and sometimes physically, in order for the economy to thrive and to benefit especially a select few. When a free market system is long entrenched, with a kind of American Dream mythology growing around it, a citizen's questioning the system or looking for alternatives becomes almost an act of sedition.

b. *For the sake of tradition.* With "The Lottery," Shirley Jackson challenges readers to reflect on the routines and traditions that we follow without questioning their origin, intent, or *economic* impact. In the story, no one can quite recall when the lottery began and what its original purpose was. To Old Man Warner, any questioning of the tradition or treating it without the proper gravity is foolish and disrespectful, even if, in the end, that tradition results in the barbaric execution of a harmless person. Almost the entire town participates in the stoning of the "winner" of the lottery, even her husband and child, without question. While we can hope that no such practices occur within our own communities, we can probably reflect on the routines and traditions that recur during our lives to see how they can cause harms about which we have been insensitive.

c. *No message here.* Too often, when readers read stories, they look for some hidden message that may not be there. A writer or artist may have produced a story, a film, or a visual image to make an impression or spark an emotional response—for example, fear, nostalgia, sentiment, joy, distress, or confusion. Very often, a film-maker will produce a "horror movie" with the intention of frightening the viewer through a strong emotional response to the perilous condition of an admirable character, or a director might immerse the viewer in a series of action-packed episodes to give the viewer a sense of the thrill of the action. Readers should keep in mind that Shirley Jackson wrote *The Haunting of Hill House*, which was twice made into a movie. Shirley Jackson's intent was to scare the heck out of the readers, not to warn the readers that supernatural elements exist in the world or some other socially redeemable message. Any reader who reads "The Lottery" in hopes of finding some deep message reads in vain; Jackson simply wanted to shock readers with unimaginably horrible scenario, what one reader called "quotidian Gothic" (Ashton, 2018, p. 269).

d. *Who knows what evil lurks?* With "The Lottery," Shirley Jackson offers some keen insights into the psychology of mob rule. The setting of the story is a town where people seem normal and decent, but in the end, they participate together in a shocking act. Every family in the town is aware of the importance of June 27. They gather together without being prompted. Every community member has a designated role in the proceedings. Once the events begin at 10:00 a.m., they proceed without interruption or interrogation. The only complaint comes from a single individual, the collective's victim. The process aligns with mob psychology or crowd psychology. It is as if the town is not a collection of individual minds but has become one mind swept up in the shared endeavor. In the enthusiasm to pursue a common goal, the participants do not pause to reflect on the merits of their mission but move forward as if they were cells joined together into one organism. Jackson saw such behavior within her own community but could see it further in political movements and in the fever to enter into armed conflict.

e. *From ritual to wretched.* Curiously, Shirley Jackson embeds several religious images in her story. The story includes town elders Mr.

Adams (as in the first human) and Mr. Graves (as in the destination from human *birth* to eternity). The act of human sacrifice and the slaughtering of a person by stoning are both images from ancient religious ritual. The wooden box that is necessary to hold the lottery is cobbled together with pieces of the original box from a distant time, as if it contains sacred relics, like pieces of the "true cross." One of the boys is Harry Jones, a common name and perhaps a "hairy" or base character, and he is joined by his friend of Dickie Delacroix, which translates to "of the cross." When you put all of these images together, what do they suggest? It seems that Jackson is not criticizing tradition and ritual in general, but the use of religion to justify the committing of the most hideous act. She suggests that humans are essentially barbaric, and their rituals, especially religious rituals, are a thin veneer for covering up their true character.

f. *Who put these guys in charge?* In the world that Shirley Jackson creates for "The Lottery," men run the whole show. The male elders protect the traditions, store the wooden box for the lottery drawing, and manage the process. It is the male head of the household who draws the lottery ticket for the whole family and thereby determines the fate of some member of the family. Of course, in the end, it is a woman who is sacrificed. When she protests that the system is unfair, she is encouraged to be a good sport. Her husband does not defend her, and her child takes up a stone to participate in the woman's execution. Jackson suggests that the sacrifice is intended to advance the welfare of the whole community, although no one can explain the connection. In her position as wife and mother, Jackson must have known first hand that women in her society were expected to sacrifice themselves for the good of others, especially men, and accept this fate as a "good sport." The story serves as an allegory for the lives of millions of women.

g. *Witness to death and destruction.* In judging this story, it is important to keep in mind that Shirley Jackson wrote it a few years following World War II. All wars are brutal, but World War II demonstrated a human capacity for cruelty and killing that has no equal, with the systematic extermination of millions of noncombatants, the vast bombing of huge populations centers, and the first uses of atomic weapons to cause unprecedented destruction, death, and suffering. Jackson would have been aware also that in any totalitarian regime in the twentieth century, children were encouraged to turn on their parents, young people embrace ideologies of hatred, and seemingly decent people witnessed mass killings as if they were on a picnic outing. One cannot read the story without attention to Jackson's reaction to the recent world war.

WHAT TO EXPECT IN DISCUSSION

As students study the views and report them to their peers, they attempt to understand the thinking behind the various critical stances for reading a text. As students all evaluate how various readers have responded to the reading, they have to answer some basic questions: In order to understand a text, must we know something about the author and the historical context for the production of the story? If we look at the story from a gendered or political perspective, are we imposing an external agenda on the reading of a text? In reading a text closely, should we confine ourselves to the features of the text alone, without regard for other texts or information? Can a story's "meaning" simply be the *effect* it has on the reader, or what Appleman (2000/2014) calls a "reader-response"? (p. 30).

Inevitably, as students report views, evaluate them, and contend with questions and challenges from their peers, they will address the questions above. Also, as discussed in greater detail in chapter 6, students immerse themselves in the procedures that can transfer to a written response: framing a problem related to interpreting and evaluating a text, representing and judging a variety of views, advancing an interpretation in the context of a conversation that includes several critical voices.

A teacher might wonder, "How am I going to construct a set of critical views for every text we read?" The answer is that this is not necessary. Of course, this book and others (Graff, 2003; McCann & Knapp, 2019; 2021) offer examples of such critical lenses. But teachers should be selective in asking students to apply a variety of lenses, with the expectation that after some practice, students will begin to recognize, and perhaps appreciate, that there are several ways to read a text and the reader should be mindful of these possibilities. In fact, if students are going to write about a text in a meaningful way, they need to be able to frame a problem by acknowledging that *other* readers have disagreed about how to read and evaluate the text.

EXPANDING PRACTICE WITH A COMPLEX TEXT

The two levels of practice described above should put students in a strong position to examine other, more complex works through several critical lenses. Perhaps after practice, students only need a prompt to look at a text through gendered, political, psychological, and historical/biographical lenses. A teacher can conceive of other possibilities for critical lenses and for texts that have long been part of the high school curriculum. For most literary works encountered in high school, there is a long critical tradition that will reveal how various readers have responded to the texts.

Consider such entrenched texts as *Romeo and Juliet, Hamlet, Lord of the Flies, The Great Gatsby, A Raisin in the Sun, The Grapes of Wrath,* and *The Crucible*. These texts readily invite consideration through several contrasting lenses. Other, more contemporary texts, such as *Beloved, The Road, All American Boys,* and *The Hate U Give,* also invite competing views. A teacher might easily imagine how readers are likely to view the texts through various lenses or check available reviews online. Whether students are reading the old chestnuts or contemporary works, they can gain much insight by looking at a text through various lenses. An awareness of competing views of a text can prompt genuine discussion and reveal the interpretation and evaluation problems that give significance to written responses. Without the experiences *and* practice with genuine discussion, students asked to participate in small groups (or whole class conversations) often begin unsuccessfully, because they have limited command of literary arguments and conventions (Marshall et al., 1997, pp. 247).

As with the two shorter works discussed in this chapter, a teacher can follow a similar sequence of learning activities that invite students to look at a text in a variety of ways. The discussion that follows will position learners to evaluate the possibilities and judge which views have merit and which views are more dubious. Students can closely scrutinize a view within a small group and then discuss the many possibilities through a whole class forum. The exploration of the many possibilities represents a genuine inquiry into literature and immerses students in procedures for analysis and critical thought.

YOUR VIEW

Perhaps you judge that students will naturally discover on their own the many perspectives from which to read a complex text. This chapter, however, recommends *specific* instructional practices that amplify the differences across a set of views (cf. Hillocks, 1999, pp. 10–19). Such emphasis encourages disagreements and fosters genuine discussion, which positions students to be able to frame the problems that become the focus for their writing. To what extent do these recommended practices seem practical and advisable to you? You might want to discuss the following questions with your peers.

1. What reservations, if any, do you have about introducing students to various lenses through which to view a work of literature?
2. What benefits, if any, do you see in instructional practices that position students to look at a text through several lenses?
3. This chapter suggests some conventional lenses: for example, political, psychological, gendered, historical/biographical. What other possibilities

can you think of, and why do you think these other lenses are too important to ignore?
4. If you were to inject some conflict into discussions about literature, how selective would you be in limiting such considerations to a limited number of texts? What texts do you think would be especially appropriate for examining through several critical lenses? Why these texts in particular?
5. If you were to introduce students to a few competing critical views, where would you find such views and how would you represent them in a way that students find accessible?

Chapter 6

Responding to Literature in Discussion and Writing

Two conventional ways that teachers expect students to respond to literature is through classroom discussion or a written assignment. For many teachers of literature, classroom discussion is the most common instructional activity, while a written response follows naturally from extensive discussion about a topic.

What some teachers refer to as *discussions* are in fact *recitations* (Nystrand, 1997). If teachers want open explorations about the meaning that readers infer from texts and about how they evaluate the quality of the writing and the thematic implications, then they want *discussions*. So, the goal is for teachers of literature to recognize the features that distinguish discussion and develop some facility at planning, initiating, and facilitating discussions. While there may be appropriate places for *recitations* as a means for assessing basic comprehension, these uses are limited and not to be confused with genuine discussions. This chapter cannot explore all aspects of discussions about literature; readers should consult the many useful and readily available resources: Applebee, 1996; McCann, Kahn, & Walter, 2018; McCann, Johannessen, Kahn, & Flanagan, 2006; McCann, Bouque, Forde, Kahn, & Walter, 2019. The first half of this chapter demonstrates discussion in action and offers some rudiments for initiating and managing discussions about literature.

Imagine two discussions—one in middle school and one in high school—to identify the patterns that teachers often fall into and that students disengage from. If you hope for classroom discussions to be more meaningful than they appear here, then it will be necessary to reflect on practice and to identify and refine the pedagogical moves that invite students to participate in discussions and that immerse students in procedures that can transfer to written responses.

Chapter 6

PORTRAITS OF TWO DISCUSSIONS

In the first instance, an eighth grade teacher poses questions about Shirley Jackson's often anthologized story "Charles." In reviewing this brief transcript, consider these questions: What is the function of asking students to respond to the literature? What should be the function? How can a teacher invite responses that will align with the goals and foster a disciplinary approach to reading literature?

Ms. Begalky: Where in the story does the author reveal that she is proud of her son Laurie?

Theo: What? His name is Laurie? That's a girl's name.

Ms. Begalky: Laurie can be either a boy's name or a girl's name. Perhaps when this story was written it was more common as a boy's name. But, back to my question: Where does the author show that she is proud of her son?

Leti: Is the author the person who is telling the story?

Ms. Begalky: Not always. But in this case, it looks like the author is the person telling the story about her own family. So, where does she show she is proud of her son? Well, let's look at the beginning of the story. What does it say?

Monica: Well, she doesn't say she is proud of him, except that he is growing up. He's wearing long pants and swaggering. What's that? Wearing long pants? Does that mean a kid is grown up when he wears long pants? Everyone wears long pants.

Ms. Begalky: At one time, boys wore short plans, like knickers, until they reached a certain age and then they were allowed to wear long pants. It's like a rite of passage, a way of showing that you were growing up. That brings me to my next question: how does the mom feel about her son growing up?

Olivia: She's proud of him?

Ms. Begalky: That's right. She is a little nervous that he is going off to school for the first time, but he seems confident and she is proud that he is growing up a bit. Now, when Laurie comes home from school, what does he report about Charles?

David: He has been bad at school.

Ms. Begalky: He is bad in what way? What specific things has he done?

Letti: He likes to talk back to the teacher.

David: He hit the teacher.

Letti: He hurt a girl on the see-saw. And he kicked a guy.

Ms. Begalky: Okay, he has done a lot of things that got him into trouble with the teacher.

Theo: She spanked the kid. How can she get away with that? The parents can sue her. And he's only in kindergarten.

Ms. Begalky: This story takes place a long time ago when teachers can administer corporal punishment. They were allowed to spank or crack someone on the knuckles with a ruler.
Theo: Did that ever happen to you?

Perhaps you can recall such exchanges in school, either when you were a student or when you tried to initiate conversations in your own classroom. You might think that most teachers of literature would avoid the kind of questions that Ms. Begalky asked, but a simple Google search of "questions about Shirley Jackson's 'Charles'" will yield similar questions, and many teachers rely on the readily available web-based resources. Often these resources share lists of questions that prompt recall of basic elements like narrative point of view, setting, characters, conflict, and resolution, without much attention to why these elements matter in interpreting and evaluating the story.

The questions in Ms. Begalky's class largely focus on recall or simple inferences, and the teacher appears to operate under the assumption that students need to command the basic facts of the setting, characters, and actions to be able to recognize the implications of the story. That may be the case, but a teacher and the learners do not have to operate from a bottom-up stance, a kind of pathfinder model (Marshall, Smagorinsky, & Smith, 1995). Often a class can begin with a complex inference question and find itself moving up and down several taxonomic levels as they explore the question (Hillocks, 1980; Hillocks & Ludlow, 1984).

Being aware of question types and the notion of "authentic questions" (Nystrand, 1997) that don't have prespecified answers is just a start. You may have noticed in the dialogue above that Theo seems determined to explore curiosities that are outside of the teacher's agenda. In fact, Theo poses some authentic questions, although the exploration of his questions may lead far away from the text. How is it possible, then, to pose "higher order" questions that do not have prespecified answers? Better yet, how can a teacher frame an interpretive problem that can engage learners in thinking both globally (considering how the elements of the text work together) and narrowly (closely examining individual elements)?

Consider a second classroom interchange below. The class focuses on Kate Chopin's very short story, "The Story of an Hour." In this case, as the opening remarks suggest, the teacher has likely prepared students in a way that is consistent with the preparatory practices offered in chapter 2. How does this second dialogue differ from the first one in this chapter?

Mr. Calloway: You may have been surprised by the ending of the story. Some of you may have been as shocked as I was when I saw Mrs. Mallard's cold-hearted reflection on her husband's death, a death in a train disaster, which must have been a nightmarish scene and a horrible way to die. In your teams, you have discussed your assessment of Mrs. Mallard's behavior, and I am interested in knowing what you concluded.

Cynthia: I don't think we agreed on anything. Robert was like you and thought that Mrs. Mallard was terrible because she seems happy that her husband died. But Veronica and I thought that it is just realistic. I can see that even if she loved someone, it was a time when men controlled everything. Mrs. Mallard wanted to be free from the control of her husband. I don't know what she was going to do, but she could decide for herself and anything could be possible.

Nancy: Our group kinda had the same ideas. Jessica and I didn't say that it was exactly a good thing for her to be happy that her husband died. But if she was like controlled like Cynthia said, then this would be the first time she was free to decide. That idea of being outside someone else's control could have been the most important thing to her.

James: Yeah, but there is nothing in the story that says that the husband was abusive or something. It says, "The face that had never looked save with love upon her." That's her husband. She is thinking about this and says that he never looked at her except with looks of love. That doesn't sound like a mean, abusive guy. Come on, you wouldn't be happy that a person who loved you died in a train disaster.

Mr. Calloway: Before we go one, James, could you point out where you quoted from the story?

James: Yeah, it's on the first page. No, it on the top of the second page. It's the first paragraph on the second page.

Mr. Calloway: And this is supposed to be the narrator telling us what Mrs. Mallard is thinking?

James: Yeah. She doesn't say this out loud, but it's supposed to be what she is thinking.

Mr. Calloway: Okay. Silvia, what did you want to say?

Silvia: You know, you could be happy to be free of someone, even if that person loves you. A person could love you or think they love you and control you all the time. When the story was written, like the man would be making all of the decisions, and she wasn't free to get a job or go after like hobbies and stuff that he didn't like or approve of. She just wants to be free to do what she wants, and his death makes that possible.

Robert: I don't know. I don't see anything in the story that says that the husband was abusive or something. Like James read, he loved his wife. That's pretty mean to want him dead, especially if she wants him out of the way to do her hobbies.

Mr. Calloway: Let me just go back to what Silvia and Cynthia and Nancy said. Just to check that I understand. So, you're saying that at the time, 1894, especially in southern Louisiana, where Chopin lived, the husband would be the dominant figure in the relationship, and he probably controlled much of what his wife could do. That could be horribly stifling for some people, so you are saying that it is not unreasonable for a wife in that condition to feel a sense of relief that her husband has died. Do I have that right?

Silvia: Are you asking me?

Mr. Calloway: Yeah, or Cynthia or Nancy.

Cynthia: Yeah, that's about right. But it is kinda complicated, like Robert said. At first, Mrs. Mallard cries and sobs when she learns that her husband has died. Here (reads): "She wept at once, with sudden, wild abandonment, in her sister's arms." That's in the first paragraph. So, she is sad at losing someone she might have loved, but she could still be relieved that she has a chance to be in charge of her own life.

Mr. Calloway: Did she love him?

Bailey: Well, first of all, could we call her Louise? That's her own name and not one taken from her husband. It says, "And yet she had loved him—sometimes. Often she had not." That's on the second page. Wait. It's the third paragraph. So, that means that she loved him but often she didn't. I know that a lot of couples have really strong feelings when they get married and then have disagreements and get angry and maybe fall in and out of love. Or, maybe the marriage was arranged. That could have happened at the time. That still goes on now.

Gina: Yeah, and in the same paragraph, it says, "What could love, the unsolved mystery, count for in the face of this possession of self-assertion which she suddenly recognized as the strongest impulse of her being!"

Mr. Calloway: Wait. Who is speaking there?

Gina: Uh, that's not Louise. It's the narrator, but the narrator is saying Louise's thoughts.

Mr. Calloway: So, what does that reveal to you?

Gina: It's like asking, "Who knows what love is?" It's like people in marriage are supposed to be in love, but who knows what that really means? And it says that so what if they loved each other, it's more important to be a free person.

Mr. Calloway: That's an interesting observation, Gina. What do the rest of you think? I am wondering what Kate Chopin's position was. Is she saying that marriage is a really bad deal for women in general? Is it a really bad deal for Louise in particular and not necessarily for women in general? Or, maybe she thinks marriage is a bad condition for anyone. What do you think?

The exchanges above are a composite of many discussions. This would be a very bright and cooperative group of high school students. But the success or failure of a discussion in response to literature isn't simply a matter of being lucky enough to have the right group of students. We can generalize about some of the basic moves the teacher, Mr. Calloway, makes to promote discussion. First, Mr. Calloway initiates the discussion by framing an interpretive problem: One would think that a spouse who finds some delight in her husband's demise would be a horribly insensitive person, unless there were certain complicating circumstances. Is Louise Mallard such a person, and what does Kate Chopin think of her? This is an open problem and a "scriptally implicit" question (Pearson & Johnson, 1978). That is, the answer is not something a reader can readily point to in the text; rather, the reader has to connect various elements in the text and draw from knowledge about how narratives work and from schemata (i.e., scripts) about human behavior, relationships, and marriage in order to construct some meaning about some cited details.

Mr. Calloway did not start the discussion cold. Apparently, he had already introduced students to the interpretive problem and gave the students time to discuss in small groups. As a result, Mr. Calloway could assume that everyone had something to contribute to the conversation. In fact, as a way to encourage broad participation, he might start the discussion with someone who has been rather reticent about contributing, perhaps with the intention of fostering some confidence in this contributor. The small group discussion allows students to prepare, including marking key passages that they could cite during the whole class discussion. So, some sort of preparation is essential. This preparation could take the form of a brief, informal written reflection, a conversation with a single partner or a discussion with two or three peers.

It is important to note what Mr. Calloway does and doesn't do. First, he doesn't respond to students with an evaluative comment: "that's right," "very good," "correct," or the many variants on approval of the response. If he had responded with an evaluative remark, he would have signaled that the conversation was no discussion at all, but recitation. A few of the most reliable respondents would have waved their hands for attention, eager for the chance to hear the teacher's approval. In contrast, Mr. Calloway responded by either paraphrasing the students' contributions and checking for the accuracy of his understanding or asking follow-up questions, especially asking students to support claims and expand their analysis for the benefit of the class. In this case, Mr. Calloway's questions were not his attempts to steer students toward his way of thinking; in fact, he seems to raise further doubts to delve deeper into the story.

Paraphrasing the contributions that others make to conversations is a powerful skill for teachers and can be practiced in almost any conversational situation, and it is a skill that a teacher will want to encourage with students. First of all, the intention to paraphrase forces the discussion facilitator to avoid evaluative remarks, unless a student offers some gross inaccuracies. In an effort to paraphrase what a speaker has said, the facilitator must listen actively and carefully. The paraphrase serves as a check for understanding; in fact, Carl Rogers (1961) suggests it is such a powerful communication tool that it could help nations avert disastrous conflicts; and being able to say back to an opponent what you understood and checking for accuracy helps us to understand what someone else is thinking but can also help a stubborn discussant see some error in thinking (Grant, 2021).

The practice of paraphrasing rather than evaluating allows the facilitator the opportunity to invite more commentators into the conversation. The teacher's move might look something like this:

> James pointed to this provocative passage: "There would be no powerful will bending hers in that blind persistence with which men and women believe they have a right to impose a private will upon a fellow-creature." He concludes from this that both partners in a marriage impose their will on another human being. James notes that Louise finds this intolerable. How do the rest of you read that passage? Is this Kate Chopin's indictment against marriage in general?

Here the teacher notes what someone in the class has contributed to the discussion, without commenting on the accuracy or merits of the contribution. The teacher then invites others to comment on the student's analysis: instead of the teacher evaluating, the teacher invites other students to comment on their peer's comments.

Teachers report that discussion is a key activity in their endeavor to teach literature, yet Nystrand (1997, 2017) reports that seldom do genuine discussions occur. If discussions are important for exploring and understanding literature, teachers need to learn and practice the moves that make a difference in shifting from recitation or teacher-dominated classroom discourse to more open, inviting, inclusive, and dynamic dialogue. As Rogers (1961) observes, anyone can practice active listening and paraphrasing in everyday conversation. The practice can not only help you refine pedagogical skills but also serve to mend relationships, and perhaps cool heated political conversations at the holiday dinner table.

An earlier publication (McCann & Knapp, 2021) offers a summary of practices to promote genuine classroom conversations about literature. A variation on that summary appears below for a quick reference. These practices apply principally to classroom conversations, but they can also serve a teacher in monitoring online discussions to "be present" in discussion forums and to help to expand thinking and keep the conversation civil.

SUMMARY OF PRACTICES TO FOSTER CLASSROOM DISCUSSIONS

- Plan for discussions by framing authentic critical problems that students can find significant and structure the opportunities for students to talk to each other.
- Pose a genuine critical problem instead of a long list of questions.
- Be sure that you provide students opportunities to get ready for discussions—by writing, by talking with a partner, or by discussing with a small team.
- Respond to students' contributions by paraphrasing what they have said and asking them to affirm or deny the accuracy of your representation.
- Call on other students to evaluate the merits of the comments of their peers.
- Ask appropriate follow-up questions that prompt students to support their claims and interpret what they offer as "evidence."
- Don't accept "I dunno" as an answer; instead, reframe questions and offer choices.
- Don't expect easy closure when discussions focus on genuine critical problems that may never lead to consensus.

The practices listed above represent skills that a discussion facilitator refines over time. As with any set of skills, these require substantial practice over time. It would not be unusual for someone to be frustrated in attempting these practices and finding a lapse into recitation and "path finding" (Marshall, Smagorinsky, & Smith, 1995). Anyone who has ever practiced a skill—learning to play tennis, learning a new language, learning to play an instrument—has experienced some initial frustration. The frustration is not the signal to give up, but to focus on the elements of the skill that require some refinement. For a teacher committed to facilitating meaningful discussions about literature, every day provides several opportunities in the classroom to work on skills in promoting genuine discussion. As Ericsson (2017) observes, practice needs to be "purposeful"—that is, practice with a conscious goal in mind and pay attention to how the practitioner is moving toward that goal.

To depend only on one's own reflections on practice can be both limiting and deceiving. It is easy to enjoy the contributions of the reliable two or three students or to be dazzle by one's own insights and judge that the discussion was great, but an objective observer might think otherwise. It is useful to have someone observe classroom discussion on occasion. The observer can check on the number of students who participated, how often students contributed, and what was the length and substance of the contributions. Did the teacher avoid evaluative responses? How often and well did the teacher paraphrase contributions? What was the function of the follow-up questions? Did the questions expand the thinking or channel students' judgments in a certain direction?

Students can also help in the evaluation of discussions. Every so often, a teacher can recruit a student to tally the number of responses and the direction of the response. Did students talk to each other or did they direct all of their contributions to the teacher? If the whole class looks at the data from this tally, what conclusions can they reach about the nature of the conversations and what suggestions can they offer to expand inclusion and make the discussions more meaningful?

If teachers are going to rely on their own reflections on practice, they should have in mind a standard for practice. How does a teacher judge that a discussion went well or not? Seeing how many students participate is one indicator, but what about the substance of the contributions? In a sense, teachers should have an awareness of a rubric for judging their behavior and the contributions of the students. When teachers listen to student during discussions, how do they judge that the contributions are "good" or "bad" or that the discussions are accomplishing what the teacher had targeted. Teachers Andrew Bouque and Dawn Forde (2019) report some useful practices for teachers and students to see what actually happens during discussions and judge where improvements are in order.

There is a good chance that teachers expect to hear in discussions many of the same intellectual moves that they hope to see in students' written analyses of literature. Can students frame a problem about the interpretation and evaluation of a text? Can students represent fairly and accurately what other readers have said about a text? Can students advance their own thinking by expressing clear claims, citing textual evidence to support claims, and interpreting the passages that they cite to show the connect to claims. Many experienced teachers are skeptical about awarding "points" for contributions to discussion, because they know that the contributions may simply be efforts to collect points and not to expand thinking about the problem under consideration. If teachers listen carefully to what students say and evaluate the contributions against a model of the intellectual moves that are appropriate for interpretation and evaluation of literature, they can adjust the discussion format and procedures to shift the discussions so that students can practice the skills that can transfer to their written responses.

WRITTEN RESPONSES TO LITERATURE

First, the quality and level of elaboration that teachers can expect in students' writing in response to literature will depend a great deal on the preparation for the reading and the substantive discussions about a text. As Johannessen, Kahn, and Walter (2009) offer in their valuable *Writing About Literature*, if students are going to write about the conclusions that they have reached about a work of literature, they need to learn the basic components of an argument. In the remainder of this chapter, we cannot replicate the valuable advice and recommended activities from the Johannessen, Kahn, and Walter text; however, it is possible to highlight some of the core principles for written responses.

Teachers should proceed with planning to help students to write logical, organized, and coherent written responses by defining for themselves what they expect to see from students when they write about literature. This process of reflection involves both task analysis and "backwards planning" (Wiggins & McTigue, 2005).

First consider a task analysis. A search online for writing prompts might offer some viable ways to prompt written responses to literature, but the results can also show how not to ask students to write about the texts they have studied. Here is one example from a website called *betterlesson.com*:

> Authors frequently use literature to express opinions on controversial topics. They usually try to make their points subtly, as overt preaching often has a negative effect on an audience. Determine the **theme** and **tone** of the story. In a well-organized essay, explain how Chopin reveals her attitudes. Use specific examples from at least two of the texts from this week.

The words *theme* and *tone* appear in boldface in the original, presumably for emphasis. Students who are expected to write in response to this prompt face a daunting task.

First, the prompt presumes that one could identify "the theme" of the story, equating theme with the moral of the story or some sort of succinct observation about life or human behavior. A student who writes about this prompt would probably suspect that the teacher has a specific theme in mind, and part of the challenge would be to deliver to the teacher what the teacher expects. An alert student would easily detect the teacher's sympathies from comments and reactions in class.

So, the writer can pick a theme—oppression, freedom, domination, feminism—and write a proposition about this. Discussion about the *tone* might suggest Chopin's position in regard to the *theme*. For example, Chopin treats the subject of the story ironically, not comically or flippantly, perhaps showing that she values freedom and disdains oppression. Following the directions of the prompt, the student is supposed to draw from a sense of the tone of the story to assign a theme and Chopin's position accordingly. The student can express a proposition about a theme that Chopin seems to embrace and then support that proposition by pointing not only to the features of the story but one other text as well.

Regrettably, the student can avoid the labor of actually writing an essay by going to the many websites that offer essays about "The Story of an Hour." A Google search for "essays about Chopin's Story of an Hour" yields 1.1 million hits. The world must be full of essays about the story. As an example, a website called "Cram" offers fifty pages of links to various essays about "The Story of an Hour," claiming "about 500 essays" in all. That's just one of thousands of sites that offer essays. Presumably, teachers will want students to write their own essays and find the effort to be a meaningful experience, connected to the shared study and discussion of the story.

Of course, preparing students to write meaningfully about literature will involve more than constructing just the right prompt. But the prompt should not be one that invites a Google search that is likely to yield lots of possibilities for downloading. The discussion excerpt above reveals inquiry into an authentic interpretive problem: How does the reader judge the character of Louise Mallard, and what would Chopin expect the reader to understand about this character? The extensive classroom discussion suggests the context for writing a response: readers disagree about how to judge Louise Mallard, and it is unclear what Chopin thinks of Louise, even if readers were familiar with several other works by the same author.

FRAMING AUTHENTIC PROBLEMS

It is common in academic writing for the writer to represent what others have had to say about the subject that is the focus of the essay. This helps both to frame a significant problem and to show the reader where the author's contributions fit into the intellectual conversation (Williams, 2004). In framing the problem to prompt the writing, the teacher can refer to the classroom discussions that revealed a variety of views. While a thesis or dissertation writer might review related literature to demonstrate the significance of the project, the high school writer can refer to the analyses offered by their peers during the extensive discussions. If, as a required part of the analysis, the teacher prompts students to represent and evaluate the opinions expressed by classmates, then there is no way to troll the web to find such an essay to serve as a model or to copy as one's own.

Considering, then, how a teacher had prepared the students for their encounter with the text, how the students might have looked at the text through multiple critical lenses as suggested in the previous chapter, and how the class had discussed the text at length, a teacher might offer the following prompt:

Directions: Many readers of Kate Chopin's "The Story of an Hour" have disagreed about how to judge its implications. Is it a feminist statement about the need for liberating women from the constraints of conventional marriages? Is it a condemnation of marriage as an oppressive condition for both partners? Is it a more narrowly focused reflection on the condition of one woman at one time in history? **Drawing from the features of the text and your knowledge about Kate Chopin and the cultural environment of her time,** *argue in support* **of a viable way to read the story and** *evaluate* **its implications.** Your completed essay should have the following elements:

- An introduction in which you acknowledge some shared understanding with your reader, frame a problem related to the reading of the story, and state a position regarding the problem you have noted.
- A review of the expressed opinions that differ from your own, fairly and accurately representing each view and explaining why you disagree with it wholly or in part.
- An argument for your own view of the story, citing key features of the text and drawing from your knowledge of stories in general, human behavior, Kate Chopin, and the times in which she lived to show how you drew conclusions about the cited details from the text.
- An evaluation of the merits of Chopin's implied position of the problem you have identified.
- A conclusion in which you restate the problem and reiterate your position.
- Precise use of language that shows that you have proofread carefully and edited as needed.

Perhaps a teacher would want to offer multiple prompts so that students have options in how they can respond to the text, but this one prompt is broad enough to allow a variety of responses.

Some teachers might prefer that students respond to the text in a less formal way and would invite drawings, collages, podcasts, or musical compositions as forms of response. Those modes of response certainly offer students the opportunities to rely on their "primary mode of learning" to respond to the text; but if a teacher aims to help students to write conventional academic essays about literature and move away from the temptations and suspect models readily available online, then the prompt above can serve as a goal and can guide the teachers to prepare learners to reach their goal.

FROM PREPARATION TO RESPONSE

Again, preparing students for writing analyses of literature requires more than framing the right prompt. But the prompt represents both a goal and an assessment. Perhaps that is a redundancy, for an assessment, in the form of a multi-paragraph essay here, expresses a goal—an explicit statement of what students should be able to do and the criteria by which they will be judged. From this goal, then, a teacher can plan the learning experiences that offer a reasonable guarantee that students will be ready for the performance.

Two forms of preparation are noted above: looking at the text through multiple lenses (chapter 5) and discussing the story extensively. The exposure to multiple ways of looking at the text exposes a problem in interpreting the story and evaluating its implications. The collisions with views that challenge one's own force the reader or discussant to account for a position and find the basis for disagreeing with someone else. As the bit of dialogue above shows, when students are discussing, rather than reciting, they explain how they have come to the judgments that they hold and they assess the merits of others' arguments. The dialogue immerses the participants, even if the participants are mostly listening to others, in the procedures for argument: making claims, citing relevant evidence, interpreting that evidence, acknowledging alternative views, and evaluating those views. The purposeful sequence serves as practice with procedures that readily transfer to the written response.

TAPPING INTO THE NECESSARY KNOWLEDGE DOMAINS

As Hillocks (1986) observes, any writing task requires students to tap into four knowledge domains. This is different from the concept of multiple intelligences. The two broad categories of knowledge are *declarative* and *procedural.* Declarative refers to knowledge about concepts and information, while procedural knowledge refers to knowledge about how to do things—for example, how to read a story or how to write a story. If teachers look carefully at the writing assignments that they set for students, they can regard those assignments from the student's point of view, considering all that the student needs to know in order to complete a task successfully, if "successfully" means producing a viable composition that can earn a good grade.

Table 6.1 identifies the kind of knowledge that a student would need to tap in order to complete the essay as prompted above. Obviously, if students are going to write about "The Story of an Hour," they need to read the story. If they are supposed to conjecture about Chopin's thinking, they need to know something about this author. Simply put, the writing has to have substance. At the same time, students need to have developed procedures for getting at what they know, sorting through it to discover what is pertinent to the current task and what is less important. But students also need to know the form that

Table 6.1 Knowledge Domains that Impact a Written Response

Declarative Knowledge	Procedural Knowledge
Have I read the story, and what do I know about Kate Chopin and her "cultural environment"?	How can I recall the story I have read, and how can I remember relevant information about Kate Chopin and her time?
What am I supposed to do? What are the features of the kind of essay the teacher wants?	How can I produce an academic essay in which I assess various views and argue for my own?

the writing should take. More importantly, students need to command the procedures that they need to produce of their own text.

Too often, writing instruction takes the form of dictating a five-paragraph structure or showing students models or "mentor texts." There is no doubt that students benefit from seeing models, especially at early stages in their development as writers, but seeing the finished product does not show learners how to produce such a composition themselves. Discussions, especially extensive discussions about genuine interpretive problems, immerse students in procedures that can transfer to their writing (McCann, 2014).

While teachers often rely on recitations as a means for checking that students recall and understand what they have read, these checks can be built into more substantive discussions that require students to support their conclusions by citing and interpreting features of a text. Interpretations often require tapping into various sources of knowledge that allow the reader to make such intellectual moves as accounting for a character's behavior, deciding how an image functions symbolically, or inferring what a reversal or contradiction reveals about an author's intentions.

So, helping students to write about a literary text begins with the preparation. The pre-reading activities can raise interpretive problems that come from a critical tradition. Pre-reading activities can also position students to make judgments about characters and to reflect on thematic implications. The activities might even motivate students to read the text. How teachers prepare students for reading needs to align closely with the expectations for written responses, as revealed in prompts and rubrics.

If teachers skillfully design and facilitate daily discussions about a text, students can immerse themselves in many of the procedures that can transfer to a written analysis. A teacher can monitor discussions to check that students practice the kind of procedures that will serve them when they write about a text. As with any writing process, a teacher can facilitate a sequence of drafting responses, reviewing, and revising. The outline below (figure 6.1) provides a simple overview of a typical sequence.

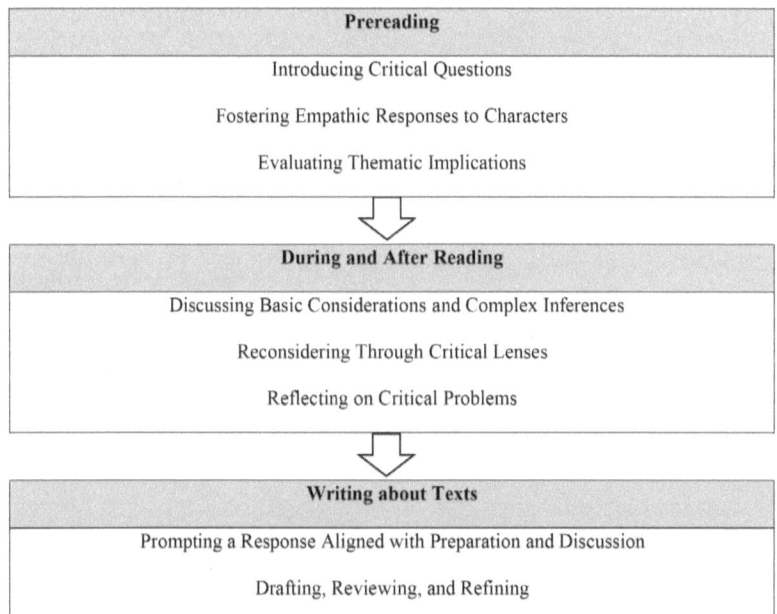

Figure 6.1 A Sequence from Preparation for Reading to Written Response. *Author created.*

YOUR VIEW

It is not uncommon for teachers to facilitate a series of discussions about a text and then offer students a set of options for writing in response to the discussion. An alternative practice is to frame a problem for writing that prompts writers to offer a response that leads to several critical views. A general prompt can allow for several possible ways of responding. The teacher's and the students' awareness of the expectations for writing about a text can set a very specific goal and help students prepare to write about the text. If discussions explore authentic questions, students can practice the analytical procedures that a written response requires. You might want to reflect on the following questions and discuss them with colleagues.

1. What distinctions do you make between recitation and discussion? What purposes do recitation and discussion serve?
2. How can you manage discussions so that they do not become narrow conversations between a few students and the teacher? How can you frame problems and pose questions that can help students to reflect on their reading and conduct extensive conversations with their peers?
3. How can you prompt students to write in a meaningful and not predictable nor duplicative style?

Chapter 7

Experiencing Literature as Performance

Teachers of literature find that sometimes the best way to enjoy a text is to experience it as performed. Certainly, plays are written to be read as well as performed, but for many, enjoying the text comes from experiencing it in live or even in filmed performance. Staged performances of both project interpretations, offering a director's conception of the work as a whole, coupled with the players' visions of the characters they attempt to bring to life. In fact, everyone involved collaborates in production—set designers, costume makers and property managers, music directors—all contribute to the effects and the core emphasis of the play.

Teachers who recognize this element of enjoyment and interpretation often try to provide students with opportunities to see and hear a play in performance. Some teachers manage field trips to a local theater; some project videos of an entire film version of a play, and some teachers carefully curate selected scenes from one or more productions. But there are also times when a teacher might want to engage learners in actual performances of given scenes in the classroom. This is certainly a worthy endeavor to bring a text to life, and the teacher need not have an extensive theater background to occasionally "put a work on its feet," whether the text is a play intended for performance, or parts of fiction narratives that invite performance as a way to envision and interrogate a scene

What follows are suggestions for fairly simple activities to help students to get on their feet before their peers and perform selected scenes from a play or novel. Students do not need to be accomplished actors—few people are, after all—but they need to feel comfortable enough to talk and move in front of their classroom audience. The performance in itself presents a vision that all viewers can question, with the interrogation focusing on the text and perhaps authorial intentions, and not worry too much about the performers' (or players') abilities.

Shakespeare's plays are the texts most popularly taught in secondary schools. Although teaching drama can be a challenge both for beginning and experienced teachers, putting on even a scene from Shakespeare's dramas may rank among the most difficult theater texts to teach. Among the difficulties include making ordinary sense of the Bard's early modern English. Difficulties begin for students in mere comprehension of the words on the page and their need to learn decoding at the sentence or line level.

Sometimes simultaneously, learners must then move toward what has been elsewhere referenced as a game called the "Snakes and Ladders of Abstraction," or language comprehension, by moving forth and back from the single word level to sentences to the global levels of meanings in the text (Knapp, 2008, p. 21). This reference has evolved from the British-named young child's toy also called (in North America) "Chutes and Ladders." These are board games where step-by-step advances in a board game may get erased by a false step (or word interpretation) that returns the player all the way to the beginning of the game (or sentence).

Another of the major problems students have is imagining in their mind's eye a given character or other characters interacting on the stage in three-dimensional space—what Bruce J. Miller (2001) calls *Actions*: "Any physical or psychological activity an actor carries out" in the service of "the through-line of action in a play" (p. 204). In fiction, actions can be referred to as "the Progression" of the plot. The progression is "the movement of the plot from beginning to end and the principles governing that movement" (Phelan, 2005, pp. 217–218).

Theater directors often informally remind actors that their *actions are essentially believing and behaving truthfully in imaginary situations*, including how a character's nonverbal actions also contribute directly to the meanings in the work. In general, all literary students of drama generally, and Shakespeare here particularly, need to acquire several actions and skills, skills to be learned *and* practiced in a classroom setting.

While some of these actions are familiar and even commonplace to acting/directing students and their instructors (cf, Viola Spolin, 1999; Miller, 2001), most English majors or just ordinary readers who have not had dramatic training will find that learning these skills, actions, and mental habits are absolutely essential in their understanding of and/or teaching about dramatic literature.

It will be helpful if the skills alluded to above are learned, attempted, and practiced, while also acquiring what most literature teachers consider their primary if not their only real job: comprehending the language of the text and inferring implications, learning the history, culture, and political basics of the time. It's of interest to know, for example, who was Queen (or King) during the times many of Shakespeare's plays were performed. What time did plays usually start during the summer?

Probably such learning seems all very familiar to most literature majors as a way of beginning a unit on Shakespeare. What IS unfamiliar to many literature readers is what is required below. It's called putting a play (or a scene) "on its feet," and doing that is no easy feat (pun intended). This chapter focuses on *some* important scenes early from one of Shakespearean plays, *Hamlet*.

We have assumed further that getting novice readers of Shakespeare hooked early in speaking the words clearly and moving on an imaginary stage purposefully. Accomplishing this makes it more likely, as so much else in literature instruction, that students will want to keep on reading the text or watching the performance to the end. Below are some sample activities to help teachers and students experience literature as performance.

While readers of this book became English teachers and/or literature majors specifically because they feel more comfortable sitting alone with a good book, the very qualities of theater texts require moving out of the armchair. Doing so, even if only in their imaginations, they then begin visualizing characters in a play moving briskly or gently and voicing loudly (or softly) their languages in three-dimensional imaginative space.

Your students (following you in this) must learn to do the following— labeled here as elements of students' learning, written as a brief set of directions (Activity 7.1).

ACTIVITY 7.1: PREPARING FOR PERFORMANCE

A. Class is divided into small groups of three and do what actors call *a table reading*. The members of the group are assigned characters (by their names) and *read out loud* their lines in order of appearance in the act and scene, completely, and then repeat, at least two or three times. The students repeat the reading aloud as part of the effort to understand Shakespeare's early modern English and to make appropriate internal translations from the Bard's language to one's own mental *equivalents* while remaining faithful to the text (cf. Pritner & Coliananni, 2001).

B. During table readings, each player (or character) tries to imagine how he/she has translated printed language into *actions*, including physical movements, by the players on stage, and can explain what was imagined to his/her classmates. Until and unless one can *see* in the mind's eye certain actions or activities, what the players/characters are doing physically and emotionally on-stage, one's understanding of dramatic texts will be limited (Ball, 1983;

McCann & Knapp, 2019, pp. 198–202). The table reading allows for a negotiation about a shared sense of the "spine" of the play and how everyone on stage contributes to this core "meaning" or effect.

C) While doing both (A) and (B) above, students *will demonstrate* how they have learned to create *actions*, moving more easily "up and down the snakes and ladders of abstraction," going from the printed word and image to the voice and activity of the player/character to the larger thematic, mimetic, and aesthetic implications of what is being perceived by the audience (Knapp & Womack, 2003, pp. 184–185).

These demonstrations may be structured as a simple sequence: repeated table readings done out loud, followed by silent movement exercises (cf. Miller, 2001, "An almost silent story," pp. 38-42), to performing a selected brief scene. For illustration, the activities below focus on a scene from *Hamlet*, employing sentences that are difficult for any reader to parse.

1. Students are to prepare *Hamlet*, Act I, scene v, ll. 1-110 by emphasizing the *language* of the scene, reading the scene and/or lines *out loud* and in its entirety at least twice. Readers are then grouped in dyads, assigning appropriate roles to each: one plays King Hamlet; the other Prince Hamlet, with each speaking *selected lines* to one another as if in conversation.
2. Each player is to read lines, one sentence at a time, to the other and do so in complete sentences by practicing *enjambment* (reading through an end line into the next), emphasizing the *verb structure* of each sentence, noting the puns, and in doing so, practicing Shakespeare's unusual syntax. An important part of this activity is the students' review of poetic terms and ordinary grammatical identifications while learning to read early modern English.
3. After students read the selected declarative sentences aloud, the other player is to ask for clarification and does so by repeating the sentence, but transforming it into the form of a question, emphasizing the *verb structure* of the sentence. Player # 1 is to respond by nodding, yes, and then repeating the transformed declarative in its entirety *as a question*. If both players have got the gist of the sentences correctly, they are to move on to the next appropriate sentence in the scene.

Both players may need a few different examples before being able to translate and so explain what they are saying to the teacher and/or to another small group. These practice sessions should be light-hearted and not stressful. No one learning to speak early modern English will do so without mistakes and missteps, just as two dancers learning to tango will occasionally step on toes. Note the two examples below.

Example 7.1, lines 53–57 (Riverside *Hamlet*). Language Interpretation

K. Hamlet: "But virtue, as it will never be moved/Though lewdness court it in the shape of heaven/So [lust] though to a radiant angel link'd/Will [sate] itself on a celestial bed/And pray on garbage."
Prince Hamlet: Do you mean that virtue will *never be moved* even if lewdness *court* it in the shape of heaven? And, on the other hand, that lust, though *linked* to an angel, will *sate [exhaust]* itself on a celestial bed and *prey* on garbage?
K. Hamlet: That's what I said, chum. Since you have the parallel antitheses of the sentences right, let's move on to the next important sentence.

Example 7.2, ll. 59-70. *Language* Interpretation.

K. Hamlet: "Sleeping within my orchard,/My custom always of the afternoon,/ Upon my secure hour thy uncle *stole*,/With juice of cursed Hebona in a vial,/And in the porches of my ears *did pour*/The leprous distillation,/Whose effect/*Holds* such an enmity with blood of man/That swift as quicksilver it *courses* through/ The natural gates and alleys of the body,/And with a sudden vigor it *doth posset*/And *curd*, like eager droppings into milk/The thin and wholesome blood."
Prince Hamlet: Do you mean that you were *sleeping* when my uncle (your brother) *stole* into the orchard and [he] *did pour* that leprous distillment that *holds* (contains) such an enmity with your blood that, as it *courses* through [your] body, it *doth [does] posset and curd*, like sour droppings into milk, your wholesome blood?
King Hamlet: That is an earful, but correct! Next important sentence?

Note above the following: (1) verbs are *italicized*; (2) line endings are marked by vertical dashes (/), and line beginnings marked by a capitalized letter of the first word; (3) the syntax is different from, and more complex than contemporary English; (4) some pronouns are specified in square brackets; (5) in this way—paying close attention to *verb structures*—Shakespeare's early modern English syntax can be made clearer to novice readers of Shakespeare.

We have selected two unusually difficult sentences to disentangle. Experienced teachers will select many more sentences that serve double employment: aid in practicing and learning to read complex sentence structure, and, simultaneously, help in moving *the progression* of the play forward, once understood. David Ball (1983) speaks of *Forwards* rather than the *Progression*, but the basic sense is the same: the audience wonders, what happens next?

Having just worked on early modern English language development skills in general, and after having practiced reading lines by Shakespeare out loud, a class can move to doing some interpretive activities (called *actions*) that will help students to understand, as they read, how scenes work in three-dimensional space. For novice readers of drama, learning how to read and comprehend, not only Shakespeare, but drama generally, requires something different from quiet reading.

What drama requires of readers is imagining in the text (by observing closely) those *movements* (*actions*) usually conceived by the play director with the players' input and enabled by the actors. Nonverbal actions as well as those coupled with voices and language are crucially important when reading or watching live theater. Reading the text silently without practicing this activity will not help most new readers *to see* the cues needed to comprehend a given scene, nor will most table-top readings aloud do that either (that is, sitting around a table, much less in a whole classroom and reading out loud but with no movement).

What Shakespeare *readers* need, ideally, is also some practice in *doing* physical movement (*actions)* in three-dimensional space. In dealing with theater work, Bruce J. Miller (2001) suggests: "Doing is far better than being; having something specific to do gives purpose to action and relieves self-consciousness as well" (p. 17).

Teachers can help—at least in early reading—by losing their own self-consciousness and by modeling for their charges how to practice, ridding one's own fears of exposure. Actors do so via training with teachers like Viola Spolin (1999), but in ordinary classrooms, interested English teachers can develop imaginative actions in ordinary readers by practicing smallish scenes from plays and, if slightly reworked, even scenes from short stories and novels.

Keys to successful practice include small audiences (groups of no more than 3 or 4), and tiny, but illuminating scenes for understanding. See below for some classic theater examples

HAMLET AND THE UNDERGROUND DADDY: DEVELOPING ACTIONS

The last scene in Act I of *Hamlet* is sometimes played comically and sometimes seriously, but either way, it sets in motion elements of the plot that ultimately complete the whole play. Hamlet has just completed a private conversation with the ghost of his father, and, as many others have discussed at length elsewhere, the son is unsure whether the visitation was of his father's spirit or an emanation of the devil (cf. Knapp, 2003, p. 205).

Either way, the son is determined to hear what the spirit has to say—even if it is a devil who "hath power/T' assume a pleasing shape" and "so abuse Hamlet to damn him" (II, ii, 603). Having learned from the ghost the sorry truth of his uncle's murder of his father and then vowing to focus upon revenge by wiping away "all pressures past" of youth, Hamlet returns to his two companions. He appears considerably agitated and he seems unwilling at first to reveal what has just transpired between him and the ghostly apparition.

It is noteworthy in the scene that when Horatio and Marcellus prevail upon him to explain his odd behaviors (repeatedly shaking hands and compulsive chatter), he swears them to silence multiple times, and Horatio confirms to the audience that Hamlet's behavior is "wonderous strange" (I, v, 163). The ghost has fled to the cellarage where it is dark (because "Matin is near"—first prayer of morning) and keeps egging on Hamlet to have his companions swear to keep his visitation secret.

Hamlet's behavior appears very nervous as he tries to satisfy his father's commands. The Prince quite literally has Horatio and Marcellus chasing from one part of the stage to another before both bow to him and his sword. The scene ends after both have sworn to Hamlet's (apparent) satisfaction, and he bids them all to leave the stage together, but not in the order of rank or social class.

As with the two scenes discussed above, this one makes far more sense when the class physically moves about the stage (classroom) to try to enact the scene. This one requires four characters (students) who may come "on stage" with photocopies of the brief scene (I, v, 114–190). Here are the procedures for enacting the scene:

1. The first four are to read lines 114–190 aloud, and then sit down. The person playing the "ghost" is instructed to move anywhere in the room and his/her only line is "swear," which the ghost repeats on cue.
2. Four more volunteers are to do the same, lines 114–190, and then ask group # 1 (above) if they approve?
3. Four more volunteers are to repeat what group # 2 did, and so on, until someone asks *why* the ghost keeps repeating "swear" *and why* Hamlet says such lines as "Hic et Ubique? Then we'll skirt our ground/Come hither, gentlemen," and "Well said, old mole, canst work i' the earth so fast?" (I, v, 156; 162).

Individual class members are to discuss with one another what they see happening and why Hamlet moves his two companions around the stage. After each group has played the scene, they are asked to explain, briefly, what *actions* are happening on stage, physically and emotionally, and how these scenes are directly related to Hamlet's motivation.

The students' explanations could range far and wide (as with the scenes above), but the crucial elements in this exercise are the following: (1) The scene has set in motion a puzzle about the references to behavior that is plain once the actions of all four players are understood.

(2) As with so much in Shakespeare (and a lot of other theater), the explanations of movement are not mentioned in the dialog but comes about through the players' *actions in conjunction with their dialogue.*

The scene seems ambiguous. Readers/viewers usually question one another, or the teacher: Is Hamlet trying to please or perhaps placate his father, and/or his friends? Students are not *told* by the teacher that there is a problem; however, most should realize, by the second or third repetition, that Hamlet's insistence on swearing does indeed seem odd, or different, or unexplained, or even "wonderous strange," both to the other characters and to the readers.

The students' speculations concerning Hamlet's (or the ghost's) motivations should center on information taken once the actions are understood. However, since this scene is also done early in the play, for most who have not previously read or seen the play, their response to what the meanings of Hamlet's or the ghost's motivations are is a variation of "darned if I know"? Such incomprehension is okay—for now.

Students' answers may be helped by keeping in mind the following actions: Of the characters on stage, who actually hears the ghost when Hamlet says, "Come on, you hear this fellow in the cellarage?" (l. 151). Does who actually hears old King Hamlet make a difference as to how the scene is played? If so, which lines suggest to the audience (or not) who, among the players, hears his word, "swear"? (l. 155).

Just as with John Keats's idea of *negative capability* [uncertainty without irritable reaching after fact or reason], it is perfectly okay for students to note a problem but also remain aware that—given the point of their reading in the text—both they and any first-time reader may *not be able* to answer these questions. What one does hope for is the students (readers) seeing with the minds' eye the physical behaviors of the players in this fragment of one scene, and then, most importantly, ask if *those actions* connect the language and action smoothly.

In order to read Shakespeare (or any theatrical text) well, students need to practice these *actions.* Student conversations and speculations among classmates who are also reading the same play (or scene) are very important. Reading out loud while trying to imagine movement on a stage requires slowing down the printed words to spoken exchanges between or among speakers—from merely reading lines to having text-related conversations.

ENVISIONING LORRAINE HANSBERRY'S *A RAISIN IN THE SUN*

Learning to read or enact a Shakespearean play for many students begins with navigating the language problems and understanding basic elements of the play. We have discussed some ways to begin to fix those issues above. In what follows with Hansberry's *A Raisin in the Sun*, we will discuss a different but equally important set of issues: how to understand characters who (typically) represent recognizable and real-seeming human beings. The actors' jobs include showing, not telling the audience that they are witnessing the staged reality of group relationships and involvement, and what they feel is what would happen if they became part of the ensemble.

Shakespeare's plays probably represent the most commonly read dramas in high schools, but consider a more modern possibility in Lorraine Hansberry's *A Raisin in the Sun*. The play may seem to be a relatively tame relic of the civil rights movement, especially when compared to the work of writers like Susan-Lori Parks or August Wilson; nevertheless, it packed a more subdued yet powerfully realistic punch to audiences of its day and to many even now. And Ta-Nehisi Coats' report in *The Atlantic* (2014) shares the historical details and the extended effect of unfair housing practices, making the Youngers' drama still poignant.

The language is a bit stylized and may sound less realistic to contemporary playgoers of realistic drama, conditioned to the frank slang and even cuss words now familiar even to middle school children. However, the power of anger and resentment of the Black characters (ca. late 1950s, and early 1960s), still resonates with passion and clarity to every audience in our own time.

The question in Langston Hughes' poem (1951) of the same title, the one Hansberry employed to stunning effect before the opening, was "What happens to a dream deferred?" A theater company might think of the question as the "spine" of the play—the central problem to which everything in the play (i.e., the costumes, the lighting, the set, the movement, the speech patterns) connects. While it remains a perennial question for working-class citizens of all colors and ethnicities, for Black Americans in 1959, and in decades following, the dream of moving upward in social living and opportunity was still "deferred" for far too many (Coates, 2014).

These were fellow citizens for whom the electronic media daily illustrated a dream they could see, but, requiring intense struggle to arrive, Hansberry's characters still had not and perhaps might not soon achieve the promise. During the next forty years and more following the era of the play, for those still trying to fulfill that dream and for those opposed, it neither festered, nor sugared over, nor sagged: too often, it exploded! And the explosions came from all sides during the last third of the twentieth century, during one of the most wide-sweeping social revolutions in America since the Civil War.

In the 1960s, the backlash of people like members of the "New Neighbors Orientation Committee" became as scary for new Black homeowners as Mama's memories of the days when "in our time we were worried about not being lynched and getting to the North if we could and how to stay alive and still have a pinch of dignity" (p. 1533). In turn, white ethnics' objections were often based upon both ignoble racist sentiments and perceived if not actual losses, in changing neighborhoods, of the newly won financial gains following the end of World War II.

The American people had to learn to accommodate and eventually accept and even welcome those who looked, spoke, and worshipped differently from one another. Being an immigrant society did not stop with the inclusion of a given social class or ethnicity but continues to this day with many of the same social tensions. President Lyndon Baines Johnson's proposed Civil Rights legislation and the U.S. Congress's enactments of civil and voting rights laws (1965–1966) helped preserve the Union's peace and diminished the explosion, at times and in places, to uneasy accommodations.

While some knowledge of American history is important in understanding the original context of the play, *A Raisin in the Sun* is essentially a drama about family. It dramatizes an underserved and underemployed African American family living on the Southside of Chicago in the years just before the American social rights revolution. The family lives in a small decaying apartment whose furnishings that "clearly had to accommodate the living of too many people for too many years—and they are tired" (p. 1508, here and below). "Weariness has, in fact, won in this room," as the opening narrator mentions quietly, because "[e]verything has been polished, washed, sat on, used, scrubbed too often."

This home holds the Younger family, Lena (or Mama), the matriarch who rules with both love and a necessary inner strength, protecting her children from a harsh and often cruel world outside. The adults in the apartment include Lena's son, Walter Lee (also called Brother), thirty-five years old, who works as a rich-man's chauffeur, and his wife, Ruth, a thirty-something hard-working and exhausted mother. Ruth and Walter Lee have raised their eleven-year-old son, Travis, in the same little apartment with Mama's daughter, a twenty-year-old college student, Beneatha.

The exposition (or explanation of the issues and conflicts within the family) is typical of a multigenerational household, with the four adults in the family each dreaming of the so-called "pot of gold," from their deceased husband's (or father's) insurance legacy of $10,000. This was a substantial bit of money in 1959, one that would be the equivalent in 2021 of approximately $100,000. For the Younger family, it is a nearly unimaginable sum, well beyond what the whole family could earn collectively in a year.

Each member of the family has a dream of what or where to put those dollars to good use. The check is, fortunately, made out to Mama actually, and so the initial struggle inside the family is who will be the one to convince Mama to make his or her dream come true. In a familiar plot development, each one—son and daughter-in-law, grandchild, daughter, and Mama—has a dream to fulfill with one check. The only adult in the household who doesn't voice her dream with increased volume is Walter's wife, Ruth, but her need is obvious from the start.

For many theater-goers, the money (the check) represents a kind of distraction, almost a red-herring, a "solution" that could solve each family member's deferred dream. However, like all distractions, the ultimate solution for almost all of them could be right in front of them and within their family, if only they could understand it. Hansberry's play, in the eyes of your humble editor-authors, can be seen in relation to Arthur Miller's *Death of a Salesman*, another play speaking as much or more to family life and dynamics than to fiscal success and American social progress.

Film versions of *Raisin* are readily available, but there is value in members of a class performing selected scenes, since the performance in itself reveals a reading of characters and the implications of the play as a whole. A teacher can proceed more easily if the class is full of confident thespians who learn from the inside out, who create characters who know what it means and feels to dream in an insecure world not of their own making. What this family does possess, not to forget, is the potential support they have right at home.

METHODS OF READING *RAISIN* FOR PERFORMANCE AND REFLECTION

So, as we readers (or viewers) settle into the tensions of the play, it might be worth pausing to sort out essential conflicts. Whether in a fictional scene or a dramatic one, the reader/viewer needs patience to understand the unfolding dynamics of the conflict. One must realize that in chronic family disputes, the pros and cons have likely already been rehearsed many times but neither pro nor con "won" the earlier versions of the debate, nor will either side, absent new and compelling information, likely will win this one either.

Like many theatrical productions, the opening act helps explain something of each introduced character's initial motivations, and also sets in motion some of the actions that make or permit something else to happen. As the class members did in the Shakespearean drama discussed above, the players (students) are to divide into groups of five (for each of the characters in Act I) and begin with the usual Table Readings.

An excellent source to move students from table readings to actions on stage is Viola Spolin's *Theater Games for the Classroom* (1986). Her initial goal is to help classroom actors get over fears of exposure and stage fright, but as *putting scenes on their feet* becomes just one more classroom activity, Spolin shows step-by-step how to help novices and nonactors learn how to enjoy reading and playing with theater stories. For a brief summary, see Spolin, pp. 190–92.

Second, students should explore the scene below, assuming that they have not yet completed the play but are witnessing perhaps one of the most common scenes in both real and fictional family life: a husband-and-wife disagreement at breakfast over what we learn is a chronic issue for all of them: choosing the best alternative concerning who gets the single check? What had been formerly just speculation is now suddenly urgent by the imminent appearance of The Check, the money than could relieve each of them of basic struggles of their poverty-dominated life.

A teacher-director should heed some realistic cautions. The actions exist is a small, cramped space (kitchen–living room combination) so the players will likely be bumping into one another regularly, by itself a minor but real irritation. All five of the characters ultimately reveal, in one form or another, what simply more usable living space would mean in their fantasies and dreams. Hence, what may seem to be a surrogate for many issues in the family also illustrates for them real-world consequences, some of which are exposed in this scene, but others will be revealed much later in the production.

This early conflict acts as a trigger, an action disturbing the status quo ante: the apparent problems raised before the real issues of the drama that compose the play's actual conflict and progression. Since any play is a series of actions, and each action builds upon the previous one, one of the most interesting methods in understanding the play is to reread it: in a sense, begin at the end and go backward (Ball, 1983). Additionally, since few modern dramas employ a narrative voice to explain who feels or dreams thoughts and emotions, reading and/or participating in a play's scenes requires us to pay close attention to both the dialogue and the physical movements in three-dimensional space made by the players.

Let's begin with a brief set of exchanges from Scene One, where knowing something about the family dynamics helps us understand familial tensions and hierarchical expectations in an ordinary early morning breakfast as they prepare for the workday (Knapp, 2003, pp. 16–18). As the family awaits for a legacy check from their late father's estate, each fantasizes about what each would be, if or when it came to her or him. Naturally, in this co-evolutionary echo-system where each contributes to and has expectations from other family members' emotional and fiscal stability (pp. 15-16), the substantial but still modest check cannot be divided well enough to fulfill everyone's dream. Therefore, familiar but ancient tensions among them arise as to who deserves it the most and why. Family breakfast is, at the moment, a time for the old round-robin of complaints: Walter wants the check to buy a business and can't understand why Ruth, his wife, seems uninterested in his dream.

Experiencing Literature as Performance 103

Below are some lines from the text, with suggestions and/or questions the director would likely pose to the players. The scene also introduces some of the major themes of the play in this initial *exposition*. Interstitial comments below and in square brackets, italicized, are the director's questions to the players in the moment. Reference to stage business is a short-hand prompt to the actor: "Physically, what are you doing that makes sense in the context of the scene or even within the whole play?"

Walter: "You see this liquor store we got in mind costs 75 thousand . . . and the initial investment on the place be 'bout . . . ten thousand each. Course, there's couple hundred you got to pay so's you don't spend your life just waiting for them clowns to let your license get approved."

Ruth: "You mean graft?"

   [With what tone does Ruth ask here? Who is she looking at?]

Walter: "Don't call it that! . . . Baby, don't nothin happen for you in this world 'less you pay somebody off!"

   [*Physically, what stage business is he doing on the word, "baby"?*]

Ruth: "Walter, leave me alone. . . . Eat your eggs, they gonna be cold."

   [What does Ruth have in her hand, and what is she doing with it?]

Walter: "That's it. Man say to his woman: 'I got me a dream.' And a women will say, 'eat you eggs and go to work.' Man say: 'I got to change my life, I'm chokin' to death, baby!' And his woman say . . . [brings his fist down on his thighs]—'your eggs is getting cold.'"

Ruth: [Softly]. "Walter, that ain't none of our money."

   [In what direction is she talking, and what is Ruth's tone, even if soft?]

Walter: [not listening at all]. "This morning, I was lookin' in the mirror and thinkin' about it. . . . I'm thirty-five years old. I been married eleven years and I got a boy who sleeps in the living room . . . and all I got to give him is stories about how rich people live" (p. 1513).

Ruth: "Eat your eggs, Walter."

Walter: "Damn my eggs . . . damn all the eggs that ever was!"

Ruth: "Then go to work."

   [Any change in her tone?]

Walter: "See—I'm trying to talk to you 'bout myself (shakes head with the repetition)—and all you can say is 'eat them eggs and go to work'"

Ruth: [Wearily:] "Honey, you never say nothing new I listen to you every day, every night and every morning, and you never say nothing new. So you would rather be Mr. Arnold than be his chauffeur. So, I would rather be living in Buckingham Palace."

Walter: "That's just what's wrong with the colored women in this world . . . Don't understand about building their men up and making them feel like they somebody. Like they can do something!"

Using some of the questions below, whose answers may help serve as guides, the *Raisin* players have selected this given exchange of a few lines and rehearse them On Their Feet. As part of a read-through of Act I, the readers and players need to know the dramatis personae, the players, by discovering who wants what in the opening, and who (or what) is blocking that specific character's needs and dreams. What types of dialogue does the character employ to overcome the obstacle(s) in his/her path to success? Here are some questions to consider while planning the performance of a scene from Act I:

1. When Ruth tells Mama that what she should do with the check is to take a cruise, was she serious? How would you know if she is serious or not? How can Ruth's attitude be conveyed in performance?
2. What does Mama mean when [the direction tells us how] she responds with "throwing up her hands at the thought" and saying "Oh child!"
3. If you were Mama, whose claim would you tend to favor? Walter Lee's? Beneatha's? Before you choose and then explain, wait until later in the scene to answer.
4. If you were in Mama's place, would you consider most important Walter's family needs and so favor Ruth's and their son Travis? Given the narrator's statement that "weariness has, in fact, won in this room," do you see a pronounced need in any one of the characters?
5. The real child in the room, Travis, asks for $0.50 for school and Ruth tells him, "Well I ain't got no fifty cents this morning." [Why, when Travis helpfully indicates some other suggestions where to get it, does Ruth tell him to "Hush up now, and just eat"? What might Ruth be feeling at the moment, relative to her conversation with Walter?]
6. Are Travis's suggestions so outlandish that the boy looks at Ruth, his mother, with exasperation? Or is there some other reason? Interesting pattern here: some male family member wants something from Ruth. What is her response like?
7. Walter enters the breakfast scene and draws a make-believe gun toward his son but then asks what the conflict between mother and child are? He asks her about why she was yelling toward the shared bathroom. In this part of the play's exposition, please look at her detailed response about a check arriving. What *is* she so upset about?
8. After her petulant explanation, Walter tells her, "You look young this morning, baby." What does he mean, and what does he imply after her response?
9. Following their exchange about Travis's fifty cents, and Walter's handing him the change, Ruth watches them both with "murder in her eyes." Does the word "murder" seem appropriate for the situation? Why would Hansberry even use it in this context?

10. As Walter explains to Ruth what he plans to do with the money he anticipates his mother will lend him, the chronic antagonism returns. What does each really want?
11. Explain what the real issues are as Ruth sees them and Walter's rebuttals. Could a first-time reader/viewer understand the argumentative position of either? Which one (or Ruth) is likely to convince Mama to hand over the whole check? How are you able to predict?
12. Is Mama herself convinced about who would get the money at the end of Act I? How do you know?
13. Moving into Act II, the viewer can see two or three major issues for the characters ahead and might like to speculate ahead of time how they'd get resolved. Once you answer these questions, what mannerisms, speech habits, and so on, can you imagine for your particular character, and what is there in the play that pushes you to try to create to use it?
    (a) Who get the check (the money) and what does he/she do with it? (b) As you look at the Langston Hughes' poem that opens the play, you could speculate about who gets, or does what, with the money, and why. (c) Does the dream dry up for one of them? (d) Does the dream "fester like a sore," or "stink like rotted meat," or sags like a heavy load, etc.? These are all the big theme questions about what to expect from the opening conflicts forward.
14. What if the play ends entirely different from the poem's expectations? We have said earlier that this is also a play about families and family dynamics. What might you expect from Beneatha, one of the two youngest characters in the play? What are some of the differences between say, thirty-five-year-old Walter's dreams and twenty-year-old Beneatha? Does either age or gender figure importantly into either's success, or not? Why doesn't she really want to marry George Murchison?
15. What about Mama's dream? What does she want and when (or if) do you realize what she's dreaming most about? Does her last conversation surprise you? Why does she end with a conversation about Walter?
16. Why does Ruth, quiet and stoic, feel pride when speaking of her husband? What has happened in the play that has changed her attitude toward Walter?

A contrast between most dramas and traditional narratives is that in drama, one thing happens and then another happens caused by the first and so on. However, in more lyric narratives and in this play, *Raisin in the Sun*, "the logic of events gives way to something else." Were you surprised by the ending? Do you or could you find out where, for example, the family is now going to live, as Mama says, "Let's get the hell out of here"?

What DO you learn about their future living situation, and, if you can't answer that question, what DO you learn about at the very end of the play? Once you have read (or watched) all of the play up to Act III. Read closely Mama's speech to Beneatha. Does the ending of the play surprise and please you or does it feel somehow less than satisfactory? Why do you think you feel what you do?

Getting students to read and understand a play with some sensitivity requires some skills particular to the genre of drama, and somewhat different from reading narrative prose. Ideally, all readers of theatrical texts would be helped immeasurably by seeing the play(s) enacted, but in the average English classroom, that ideal is not always possible, and, given time constraints in many classes, not likely even in an age of readily accessible electronic media.

So, the next best course of action for the average teacher is to instruct his/her charges into at least some of the basic activities and languages that are commonplace to those with theatrical education. This chapter focuses on capturing students' interests by emphasizing the opening act and a selection of early scenes in the play. These include attention not merely to the dialogues of theatrical texts but to those actions (including physical and psychological actions) requiring realistic imitations of imaginary circumstances.

These theatrically based skills can also help—with some adjustments—the reader of prose fiction to imagine scenes from a novel, for example, by paying more attention to the dialogue, and a little less at first to the narrative explanations while trying to unravel apparent authorial intentions of such dialogue. Then, having understood the conversations in the text, reintegrate the narrative overviews back into the dialogue, comparing and contrasting the reader's intuitions with the presumed authorial voices. Most of those who are experienced readers of drama and fiction have been able to picture in the mind's eye how a scene unfolds, but the teachers' jobs are to help our students do so with the ultimate goals of reading for pleasure and understanding.

An earlier work (*Teaching on Solid Ground* [2019], Appendix C, pp. 169–172) describes a scene from *Harry Potter and the Sorcerer's Stone*. The scene between Prof. Severus Snape and Harry Potter during a supposedly academic discussion of the Dark Arts offers a possibility for enacting a portion of the narrative in the classroom. A teacher using this scene as a dramatic conflict could easily cut and paste some of the exchanges between Snape and Harry into a class in character analysis. Both the viewer/reader and Harry are puzzled by Snape's hostile and almost irrational attitude toward a young student on the first day of classes. Why does he criticize Harry for not knowing the very materials he is there to study and learn, and why do so on the first day? Why does Harry finally respond with what Snape calls "cheeky behavior"? These characters interact is oftentimes puzzling ways through all seven of the volumes of the narrative. This scene makes for interesting dramatic dialogic exchanges, albeit not very good examples of classroom pedagogy. Similarly, teachers can select scenes from novels and short stories to perform, especially when the selected scenes represent keys for understanding the work as a whole.

YOUR VIEW

A common model of a literature teacher is one who assigns students to read a text and then facilitates some form of discussion about the reading. Few English teachers think of themselves as acting coaches. This chapter encourages teachers to help students to perform selected scenes from literature as a means of delving deeply into characters and thereby explore thematic implications. Talk to your colleagues about the value that you and others see in exploring literature through performance.

1. While *Hamlet* is sometimes considered too difficult for some high-school students, what has been your experience with teaching it? Would putting selected scenes "on their feet" help your particular students begin to build a better understanding of the play?
2. Compare/contrast *A Raisin in the Sun* (1959) to the follow-up production produced some fifty years later, called *Clybourne Park* (2010). Given the differences you may recognize between the two plays, suggesting cultural developments between the 1960s and the period between 2000 and 2020, would these two plays taught together be helpful for your students? If not, what do you see are problems? Where do you see differences in performance and in implications?
3. Most theatrical productions do not feature a knowledgeable narrative voice explaining the motivations of characters or explaining why a given player acts as he/she does. Can you think of a scene in *Raisin* where a narrative voice might have helped your students understand a character's motivation with greater nuance and clarity?

Chapter 8

Fostering a Reading Habit

Somewhere, someone must have mentioned or created an old saying that bad habits are hard to break, but incurring good habits are, in their own way, just as difficult to acquire. For many literature teachers, helping adolescents to develop habits of reading literature is almost as tough as getting them to set down their smartphones for extended periods of time. Contrasted to the purported solitary nature of reading a good book, the lure of chatting with friends makes acquiring a regular reading habit as difficult to acquire at times as a healthy diet complete with green leafy vegetables and small dessert.

A regularly established reading habit is one that is done both in a solitary and in a social context. Good literature teachers know full well that sharing insights about characters in a book or debating about a narrator's more controversial beliefs about the nature of friendship or love or loyalty can be as simulating and, at times, as contentious as any social media exchange about relationships, betrayals, slights, and intolerable attitudes and behaviors.

The previous chapters in this book offer guidance to English language arts teachers in their effort to teach adolescents how to read literature closely and critically and with some enjoyment. This book and a previous one (McCann & Knapp, 2021) propose that when students move from primarily plot issues and simple what-happens-next anticipations to learning even elementary considerations of how narrative texts are constructed, they learn to develop the procedures necessary for reading a text closely and critically. When done habitually, especially in collaboration with peers, learners' emotional and cognitive enjoyment of the experience of reading literature increases dramatically. How will the teacher know his/her students have learned a little something of literary textual constructions? When, after painstaking efforts to help students to improve their proficiencies in reading literary texts, can teachers watch their charges' willingness to pick up a novel or play and read it independently? The authors here ask teachers to think about and then develop some possible ways to encourage students to read literature on their own and thereby foster a lifelong reading habit.

What must a teacher do to encourage regular reading habits, including among those who previously found little enjoyment in close reading of literary books, and then to reinforce the habits of those who already do find pleasure in reading complex narratives? After many years of working with students whose reading habits fall within a broad, the authors have noted four general approaches teachers have taken to encourage on-going reading of literature. However, individual students are often diverse enough so that any one type of pedagogy may, or, spectacularly, may not, work with a given person or class. As always, it is best to proceed based on the teacher's knowledge of the learners and to adjust based on the perceived responses of the students.

Some scholars have proposed that adolescents are likely to read and write on their own, if only teachers would get out of their way and allow the learners to choose what they want to read and what they want to write (Smith & Wilhelm, 2002; Wilhelm & Smith, 2014). Those scholar-teachers believe that the *assigned* reading of *teacher-selected texts* actually discourages students from developing an enthusiasm for reading literature. What, then, are the alternatives, and what is a teacher to do when there is an expectation for holding students accountable for having read some significant literature? Four approaches have become popular for integrating independent reading into the otherwise teacher-dominated instruction in the reading of literature.

COMMON APPROACHES TO PROMOTING INDEPENDENT READING

The following discussion describes common attempts to fostering independent reading of literature, accompanied by an assessment of the intended benefits and the possible reservations. Teachers can choose an approach that is most appropriate for the instructional context and for the way in which they generally operate in the classroom. The context would include a consideration of who the specific learners are and the demands of the instructional program at the school.

Free Choice Reading

Some teachers encourage students pick anything they want to read, with perceived quality of reading as a secondary consideration. Students may read as much as they care to read. This policy would include class time set aside each week for free reading in contrast to direct instruction concerning those class member's selected texts. Teachers who take this approach might have small classroom libraries, with lots of paperbacks and a variety of magazines. Perhaps the teacher or a librarian offers brief book talks to foster some enthusiasm for reading selected titles. Of course, students can choose their own books from the local library or from their home collection or rely on an e-text on a tablet. The idea is that students select what they want to read.

The usual protocol in such a structure is that the teacher reads silently along with the students, which of course sets an example and affirms the positive nature of reading. The assumption is that when students simply read for a sustained time, over time, they will grow as readers. Under such circumstances, teachers are unlikely to make any attempts at having students document how much they have read or report in some way about what they have read. These attempts at "grading" the drive to have students enjoy their reading would undermine the whole point of the routine.

What are the possible limitations of this approach? The first, of course, is accountability, for those teachers who must be concerned about how they use instructional time and measure the impact of the instructional program. How does the teacher know that students are actually reading, even when class time is protected for sustained silent reading (SSR)? Students may have books open in front of them and actually appear to be looking at the pages, but it is hard to tell if they are actually reading. Furthermore, how does the teacher know that students' reading proficiencies are improving as a result of this effort?

Hence, one popular argument against free choice states, therefore, that few if any teachers have plain evidence, beyond anecdotal impressions, of the improvements made by an individual. In a book titled *Free Voluntary Reading* (2011), Stephen Krashen argues the opposite: pointing to thirty years of his research (Krashen, 2007) with evidence that fifty-one of fifty-four studies, SSR did as well or better as a strategy for improving reading comprehension than comparison approaches (pp. 1 & 14).

Krashen offers a mix of forty-three anecdotal and empirical studies, many of which are his own, to suggest a variety of finding: for example, that approximately 90 percent of students do read during SSR; that SSR is more successful if materials are available in the room and so not require students to bring their own reading; that those who read more have better vocabularies, exhibit greater grammatical competence, and so on (2011, pp. 4–5). That all sounds very promising.

However, in a separate work, Gary Weissman (2016) succinctly argues that "in reading a work of literary fiction, one seeks to construct and understand a story written by someone else, the author of that text; in writing (one's own) interpretive analysis of that work, one seeks to construct one's own story about the text and its meaning" (p. 7). Weissman labels such writings as "'rewritings,' and different from earlier theorists like Barthes" (p. 7). The differences between Krashen's and Weissman's arguments about the influences of writing instruction on habitually continuing to read, are, for our purposes (establishing a reading habit), can only be labeled inconclusive.

The question still remains: how can the average literature instructor know with some level of confidence that individual class members have read a substantial amount of literature and gained anything, including enjoyment, from their experiences? Students may claim to have read many pages but with scant recall. See, for example, the Woody Allen's famous story about his speed-reading class. Allen claimed that he had completed Tolstoy's *War and Peace* in one night. When asked about proof, he said only "Well, it was about Russia." Presumably, teachers will want students to gain more from their literature experience, whether they are reading with speed or with a crawl.

Free Choice, with Some Accountability

In a variant on the first model of instruction, students may select their own reading materials but must account to the teacher in some fashion about what they have read, what was important, and why they liked (or disliked) what they consumed. Such accountability may take a variety of forms and constraints ranging from detailed "reading contracts," where students agree ahead of time to X or Y numbers of pages a week, including reports to the teacher, either written and/or oral, and of Z number of issues or themes and/or details of one or more characters. Such reports might be in patterned formats (e.g., structured note-taking) with explicit bits of textual evidence to support students' claims.

These types of contracts are typically not terribly popular with many students, since they really are often merely hybrid books reports or tedious accounting measures. For students, completing contracts may become a tedious search for details rather than stimulating exchanges of analyses and arguments about character's values and ethics. Nonetheless, fulfilling contracts gives teachers and students explicit goals to meet and concrete evidence to support actual fulfillment.

A second variation of accountability might include regularly scheduled "conversations" with the teacher during class time while the rest of the class is busy with writing and/or reading on their own. This type of reporting differs substantially in the sense that the initial verbal-only exchanges take place among a few students together, and the teacher, over fifteen minutes, a lengthy time for a small-group conference during a forty-five-minute class. If most of the readings come from a collection that the teacher has already read and knows well, a few minutes of spontaneous conversation is enough for the teacher to make an informed judgment: has the reader done a good enough job of reading to conduct a mutually satisfactorily reader's conversation with both the teacher and/or among the one or two classmates present?

If the brief conversations serve as an informal assessment, that assessment might include, at the simplest level, the following: Has each of the students read the work well enough to be able to answer early basic and randomly generated questions about the literary work? From that level, the teacher might ask about the thematic implications, character analyses, narrative viewpoints, and lyrical passages worthy of further detailed exploration—until either the material, or the time for chats, or the students were exhausted. The second part of the evaluation is an assigned piece of writing. As the authors have detailed in earlier chapters, the teacher might check that each student, at some near-future date, is able to write an argument or analysis about the work that has grown out of the individual or small group "conversations." While time-consuming, this level of accountability can be as granular and as reliable as anything short of a lengthy paper assignment or a particularly detailed examination.

One of the authors had previously conducted a four semesters' trial of such an approach inside a high school and found it quite useful in allowing the teacher to judge who did the readings faithfully (Knapp, 1984). Typically, it took only two or three conference rejections of reports before students realized that their usual tricks could not work on one who had already read the books in the conversation. What was even more interesting was the hoped-for ultimate consequence: the rest of the students in class were all reading during a fifty-minute period; and, with no evasion possible, eventually most students actually began reading and, wonder of wonders, they found themselves enjoying their tasks—often to their great surprise.

The key difference between the first and the second accountability attempts is that the teacher's punishment and admonishment were absent. Students struggling to read or needing encouragement to develop their skills and habits further were simply asked to return to their seats in classes or in student halls and try again. Separate time was made available, when possible, to discuss in private what the problems in reading were, whether the material was unappealing, and what other reading choices were possible? The key was a note of good-natured try-it-again rejection rather than angry red marks on a report. Indeed, some students fashioned a poster over that part of the classroom (near the door) where conferences were held. It read: "Abandon all hope, ye who enter here'!!" and followed one small group's attempt at meeting a dare to read Dante's *Inferno*.

Limited Reading Choices from a Curated List

This variation puts the onus on a teacher to have not only read in detail all the works on the list but to find and then select items on the list that would appeal to a varied group of adolescents. Additionally, selecting some level of quality of writing is a difficult task for many teachers. What would likely be a productive mechanism for the selection process? Would the teacher (or even a select committee of teachers) want to select books on the basis of popularity? Some books tie are tie-ins to movies or popular programs from streaming services that may find a wide adolescent audience but are not only, at times, unbearably juvenile but maintain a narrow range of storylines. At least one of the reasons teens select books to read have as much to do with their seeming novelty and the exploration of worlds and human behaviors they were hitherto unfamiliar.

The second problem is that corporate profits often drive story selection. Many adolescents remain unaware of how programmed many of their choices are, especially those based on marketing surveys ranging from clothing and fashions, music, films and book selections to the latest film and TV stars' opinions of all of the above. For teachers in their thirties and forties, to resist or even rise above such pressures is sometimes difficult.

Those of us teaching in the schools during the rise of the *Harry Potter* series of seven novels may recall how popular the first two novels were, yet also remember how some adult readers shuttered at how the badly written earlier ones were. J. K. Rowlings' mixed metaphors and sentences wandering hither and thither gave the famous literary critic Harold Bloom (2001) the vapors. And at that point, fewer than three of her novels had been published; but, as many would now argue, she did learn how to write—at least more literarily—and her book sales, mostly to adolescents, did make her one of the wealthiest women in the Western world. Something about her characters' ordinariness along with their sense of agency in the face of evil adults and sometimes hapless teachers sparked young readers' interests and those of many sophisticated adults as well. For teachers to have quarantined her novels on the basis of their presumed lack of quality alone merely points to the elusiveness of many adults' (then) ahistorical judgment.

So, in brief, curated reading lists depend heavily on the quality of the curators. As the ancient Roman Senators used to speak in Latin when ensuring the safety of their emperors: "*Quis custodiet ipsos custodes*," via the Praetorian Guard, or, in English translation: "who guards the guardians?" Students may wonder about their curators: Who curates the curators?

With free reading from a teacher-selected list, accountability issues remain. Students might be asked to write conventional book reports about what they have read. Teachers may add their own specifications as to what and how they expect their students to report, but the system itself has little to specify the nature of the review: A written summary of the text? A brief biography of the author and why knowing about him/her informs the reader about the book? An analysis of a given character or a detailed scenic analysis? A thematic survey of the whole work? Perhaps the reports can take the form of podcasts, made available to all students to spark interest in other titles. Usually, the teacher will decide upon just how tight or loose the reports must be.

Literature Circles or Book Clubs

A fourth common approach to encouraging students to read often, widely, and more deeply is one that literate adults pursue after years removed from the formal structures of school. However, the model also works with adolescents. In organized classes, students are divided up into affinity groups where all members read the same novels, plays, or authors. Given certain organizations models in some classroom, individuals are assigned by the teacher a variety of roles: one is a reporter, a second a judge, a third a moderator, and so on. For some classes, teachers will be less formal and allow group roles to form naturally.

While the structures sometimes work with certain groups, the organizational pattern is usually imposed and, as such, not all members of the group are comfortable or happy with the choices they are handed. Beginning teachers may also mistake the organizational label for the actual practice of how to carry out their assignment. That is, students need to receive some training on how to act, both responsibly and diplomatically, when effecting their roles. Typically, a teacher will model with a student to demonstrate roles in the reading circle.

The end result of a round of "Lit Circles" also needs to be spelled out ahead of time. What constitutes a successful or even partly productive session of the circle? How does the teacher assess each member of the group as well as the unit as a whole? Should silent students (who may or may not have done the reading) be given the same grade as those who enthusiastically joined in discussion of a book they obviously know well? How do such activities help almost everyone is class get enthused about further reading?

For Lit Circles enthusiasts such as Harvey Daniels (2002), the core attraction of the structure is that students have choices—in the books to discussion, in the roles to play, and in the conversations they have. In high school, the teacher might limit the text choices so that each group explores a text that is conceptually or thematically connected to the texts that the whole class has been discussing together. Another attraction is that there are structured opportunities for each team to share their reading with the rest of the class. This sharing might spark some interest across the class. Some teachers might shift or rotate groups so that students read two or three of the titles (as in an adult book club) across a semester.

The options for independent reading described here are limited to just a few. Creative teachers and their students can probably find other possibilities.

There doesn't seem to be one approach that fits all classes in all contexts. The theme here is that students need opportunities to read on their own and to share their enthusiasm, or sometimes their disappointment, with other readers, just as one would in a reading club. There are abundant evidence that the more students read, the better readers they become, and perhaps better writers, discussants, and thinkers. Without worrying too much about reading in a way and to a degree that is easily measurable, teachers should seek ways to promote the independent reading of literature, and thus foster a lifelong reading habit.

YOUR VIEW

Perhaps you or a colleague have already experimented a bit with some form of independent reading with your classes. These attempts might have sparked students' enthusiasm, or they might have been questionable uses of class time. What seems to work, and what seems to be rather fruitless? You might benefit from discussing the following questions with a colleague.

1. What do you enjoy reading and how often to you tell your students about your personal reading tastes and why you like your choices? Where might there be a place for students to share their assessments of books that they have particularly enjoyed?
2. What works of print fiction or film now seem popular with your students? Can you list a few book or film titles and have you read/viewed them?
3. If you or a colleague have ever integrated an independent reading component into a class, how did the effort work? What were some shortcomings? How could the effort be improved?

Once you have completed the reading of an assigned text, how could you structure a forum for students to talk candidly about what they liked and didn't like and whether or not they would read another book by the same author?

Chapter 9

Connecting Texts in Coherent Inquiry Units

The previous chapters discuss and illustrate how to teach specific aspects of reading literature. The illustrations focus on individual works of literature. But any learner looks, consciously or unconsciously, for connections or coherence among the many texts that they are asked to read for class. Readers want to know how the current reading connects to what they already know, and they want to know the purpose for a prolonged investment of cognitive energy in working through a complex text. Too often, the literature curriculum in a school will be a disjointed and eclectic mix of texts, so that learners might read some lyrical poems on Monday, an excerpt from a memoir on Tuesday, a "classic" short story on Wednesday, and the beginnings of a novel on Thursday and Friday, all without any scaffolding or clear connection.

The disjointed nature of the curriculum is the product of the way in which texts are selected by teachers and approved by school boards. Some teachers will cling to the works of literature that they encountered in high school and feel a responsibility to protect. Other teachers will select texts that they judge will be well-received by adolescents. Teachers in some schools will seek to diversify the authors to whom they expose students. In other schools, teachers might look for texts that might help students to cope with the many difficulties that all adolescents face and the serious challenges that certain populations of young people encounter.

The focus on an evaluation of each work of literature without regard for its possible connection to other related works is a bit like building a meal menu by simply selecting items that you like, without regard for some balance or interaction, nor a regard for the people you might be feeding. Following that analogy, a meal might consist of pasta, rice, and mashed potatoes, or cookies, cake, and a hot fudge sundae—all great by themselves, but questionable as a balanced meal in which the connections or interactions enhance enjoyment and support many benefits. And the choices might be great for the chef, but a distasteful disappointment for the diner.

So, in a sense, let's turn the development of the literature curriculum around. Instead of selecting texts that appeal to you by themselves, consider a focus on an overarching concept or compelling problem that can resonate with adolescents and offer a point of entry into exploring a complex work of literature. For example, imagine a literature-based curriculum that focuses on the concept of *justice*: How does one define *justice* and distinguish it from *revenge*? Or, a curriculum team might connect all elements of literacy study around the concept of *monsters*: Why do writers invent monsters as characters in their narratives? How can readers or the characters in literature reliably identify the monsters? How can we explain why apparently normal and decent human beings commit appalling acts, especially acts of violence? In contrast, a group of adolescents might find it compelling to explore the concept of *romantic love*. What is it? How is it different from infatuation or friendship? Whoever loved who loved not at first sight? How likely is it that love will result from an arranged relationship?

LITERATURE STUDY THAT ENGAGES LEARNERS

If we care anything for the experience that students will have in our classrooms, we should consider that all human beings want to feel competent, have some sense of autonomy, and experience a sense of community with peers. It seems that a conventional curriculum that assigns students to read complex texts without any preparation, quizzes the learners to reveal those who stumble with recall or inferencing, and provides few opportunities for genuine discussion with peers will be the opposite practices that motivate and satisfy learners. In fact, beginning teachers might consider how they compromise the forming of a positive rapport with learners by assigning them difficult reading tasks without preparation, quizzing them to document their inadequacies, and forcing them to endure presentations and recitations.

An alternative path is to begin with the consequential concept or compelling problem and then select and sequence the readings to support a rich line of inquiry. Of course, teachers will want to expose students to quality literature (cf. McCann & Knapp, 2019), but teachers might also consider how any selected work of literature will contribute to the inquiry into a consequential problem and will connect to other works of literature as part of an extended conversation (cf. Applebee, 1996). Cognitive science offers two important principles that support the effort to construct a coherent literature curriculum: (1) Learning involves an effort to make connections, especially to connect new knowledge to the information and concepts already stored in memory.

(2) The connections involve the links across works of literature; but the unified line of inquiry also integrates reading, writing, speaking, and listening activities so that these reciprocal language processes support each other.

You can find in this chapter a sequence for constructing a coherent conceptual unit of instruction with literature as the core element. For more detailed guidance on how to construct such units, we direct you to Peter Smagorinsky's *Teaching English by Design* (2018). Smagorinsky acknowledges an indebtedness to Hillocks, McCabe, and McCampbell's *The Dynamics of English Instruction* (1971).

A beginning point is deciding what will be the concept that will engage students' interest and commitment to inquiry for several weeks. McCann, Kahn, and Walter (2018) note several possibilities for discovering the issues and problems that learners find consequential: surveying learners, examining the recurring themes in popular young adult literature, or surveying the recurring topics in college newspapers' online editorials and opinion pieces. Perhaps it is possible for a teacher with a long history of work with adolescents to select accurately what a particular class of learners will want to investigate. In reality, a teacher might be forced to work with the literature that other teachers have selected over the years for a particular course. It is still possible to reflect on the connections across the texts to design the sequence of study to explore the texts as they contribute to investigating an overarching problem or concept. Ideally, though, teachers should be mindful of the kind of problems and big questions that adolescents find significant.

Peter Smagorinsky's "Virtual Library of Conceptual Units" reveals many examples of literature-based inquiry units and offers teachers possibilities for the kinds of concepts that learners are likely to find compelling (http://www.petersmagorinsky.net/Units/index.html). Another good source for model units is Forde et al.'s *Inquiry Units for English Language Arts* (2020). Consider the possibilities listed in table 9.1 for some overarching concepts and related questions. One of these might serve you or a curriculum writing team in developing a literature-based unit of instruction.

A BREAK FROM TRADITION

Imagine a typical tenth-grade literature curriculum. Someone has determined that students must be familiar with Greek and Roman mythology, noting that some common allusions and vocabulary draw from ancient myths. The curriculum, then, includes Edith Hamilton's *Mythology: Timeless Tales of Gods and Heroes*. Another teacher lobbied for the inclusion of the reading of a Shakespeare play, so a committee agreed that *The Merchant of Venice* might be appropriate for tenth graders. Of course, *To Kill a Mockingbird* has long

Table 9.1 Concepts and Questions for Inquiry Units

Concept	Essential Questions
American Dream	When politicians or commentators speak about "The American Dream," what do they mean? To what extent is there really such a thing as a common "American Dream"? If there is anyone who is systematically blocked from realizing "The American Dream," how is such obstruction possible?
Coming of Age	How do we know when someone is "grown up"? What are stages of development into maturity? What are indicators of maturity? What experiences help one to mature?
Duty and Liberty	To whom, or to what entities (country, family, organization), do we owe our duty to serve? When, if ever, must someone abandon the right to liberty in order to honor a sense of duty?
Equity and Democracy	What does *equality* mean, in the sense *All men are created equal*? How can you distinguish *equality* from *equitable*? Must we treat everyone as an equal under all circumstances? If there are exceptions, what are they? How is it possible to enjoy democratic experiences and processes and not treat everyone as an equal?
Errors and Redemption	How do our recognized errors and shortcomings compromise our sense of well-being and contentment? How can a person recover from a significant mistake or from a pattern of bad decisions to lead a more constructive and purposeful life?
Freedom	Considered with all the elements of life that you value, how highly does *freedom* rank, and why? If *freedom* does not mean that individuals have no restrictions whatsoever on their behavior, what are the limitations. What freedoms are protected, and where is freedom understandably limited?
Hero's Journey	What is the typical structure and movement of a hero's tale? What is a *hero*? What societal values does the hero represent, especially in contrast to the villain or monster? How do heroes enjoy some form of supernatural aid, and why is the aid provided? How is each of us a hero in some way? How is the hero tale a kind of "wish fulfillment dream," one that seems to be shared by all humans?
Identity	How does a person form a sense of identity? What factors influence identity formation? Why is it important to have a keen sense of identity?
Justice	What is *justice*? To what extent are justice and fairness the same? Can there be *justice* without *equality*? What is the difference between *justice* and *revenge*?

(Continued)

Table 9.1 **Concepts and Questions for Inquiry Units** (*Continued*)

Concept	Essential Questions
Love	What forms of love exist, and are they all essentially the same?
	How do humans know that they are "in love"?
	How is *love* different from *friendship* or other close human relationships?
	How important are loving relationships?
Monsters	Why do writers create monster characters (e.g., dragons, ogres, beasts) in our literature? What is the function of such monsters in the narratives?
	How can someone recognize a character as a monster?
	What makes it sometimes difficult to recognize a monster?
	What causes an apparently normal person to act in a monstrous way?
	To what extent is there a kind of monster in all of us?
Outsiders and Others	What are some examples of people who are perceived as the "others" within a society?
	How does the labeling of someone as an *outsider* affect the human psyche?
	How do some humans remain resilient and confident in the face of being perceived as outcasts or "others"?
Perception and Reality	To what extend can we trust our perceptions, especially our perceptions of other people?
	When we misjudge others, what causes this error, and what harm results?
	To what extent is there a shared, objective reality?
	How can we guard against misjudging others?
Privacy	How important is it that our privacy is protected?
	What threats are there to our personal privacy?
	To what extent do we live in a "post-privacy world"?
	What harms can result to invasions of our privacy?
	To what extent are we willing to surrender some privacy in order to protect our physical safety?
Rebellion and Civil Disobedience	When, if ever, can a person break a rule or law and still be acting in an ethical way?
	How can a person justify civil disobedience?
	When do conditions become so intolerable that people find rebellion necessary?
	What is the place of the *rebel* in civil society?
War and Peace	How do wars occur?
	Are wars ever justifiable? If you can think of a "just" war, what is it, and how can you judge it to be "just"?
	How do wars bring out the worst and the best in humans?
	What are the devastating effects of war—on persons, economies, and cultures?
	How, if ever, can wars be avoided in the future?

been a staple of the curriculum, so that stays in place. Yet another teacher saw a need to include a "more contemporary" text, so the committee selected Marjane Satrapi's *Persepolis*.

Perhaps the committee members saw how the various texts connect, maybe through an inquiry into concepts of *justice* and *prejudice*. But the texts were not selected because they represent a rich and engaging inquiry into compelling problems that invite extensive discussions and elaborated writing about the texts and their thematic implications. It is as if the members of the committee began with the default that *To Kill a Mockingbird* is already in place, and so they asked, "What next?" That's hardly a way to construct a curriculum that is engaging for learners, that will invite the reading of selected texts, and that will foster a sustained enthusiasm for reading literature. The guide below offers a blueprint for constructing a more cohesive inquiry-based unit of study.

CONSTRUCTING THE UNIT

Constructing Coherent Conceptual Units of Instruction (see the summary below) provides an overview of a curriculum development process. This overview is consistent with the advice and descriptions offered by Peter Smagorinsky (2018). Again, Smagorinsky acknowledges the influence of Hillocks, McCabe, and McCampbell's *The Dynamics of English Instruction* (1971). The outline below is also influenced by the work of David T. Anderson of Hinsdale South High School, Clarendon Hills, Illinois, and Mary Howard, Community High School, West Chicago, Illinois. Constructing Coherent Conceptual Units of Instruction provides a "big picture" view of the curriculum design in broader chunks rather than a series of steps.

This plan for unit development can serve preservice teachers who will be screened for their teacher license worthiness through a teacher performance assessment. The unit overview identifies the many elements of instruction that must align. While the overview offers a plan for unit development, some elements invite especially close attention. We recommend that the work of Jane Feeney Kade (2020) offers an especially strong model for an inquiry-based unit, and she reveals the thinking that drives the instructional design.

RATIONALE

Teachers need to have a strong *rationale* for anything they teach. Some experienced teachers work confidently with texts and activities that they have engaged with for years, but early career teachers especially need a stronger justification than "because it's in the curriculum." When a teacher operates on the basis of a perceived obligation to conform to an established curriculum or to do what other teachers are doing, the teacher operates on shaky ground, and adolescents know it. Teachers can proceed with greater confidence and sense of mission when they can readily explain to someone else why it is important to facilitate inquiry into a compelling concept and how that concept is rich enough to sustain inquiry and connect several significant texts.

Some students will wonder, if not say out loud, "Why do we have to read this stuff and do these activities?" If teachers are going to develop positive rapport with learners—a consideration upon which all else depends—then they need to be able to anticipate the question and respond with something more than "because I told you so" or "because the curriculum requires it" or "it will be on the State exam." When teachers have an unshakeable commitment that the problems to be explored in an inquiry-based literature unit are of critical importance, then students can appreciate this sense of purpose and are likely to join in enthusiastically, or at least cooperatively, in the shared investigations.

The rationale for a literature-based unit should address these basic questions: What are the problems represented by the concept? Why are the problems significant for anyone to study? Why would a specific group of adolescents find the inquiry engaging? How is the inquiry into the central concept developmentally appropriate for a given group of learners? How is the concept or central problem rich enough to sustain inquiry over several weeks and link together several significant literary texts?

TARGET OUTCOMES

The identification of the central concept will lead the teacher or a team of teachers in establishing learning targets and selecting the materials that will support inquiry. The learning targets must be situated within the particular grade, group of learners, and learning goals for the school. Generally, the *learning outcomes* should identify the students' performances that result from the learning during the unit of study. So, any statement of a learning target should note what *learners* will do (e.g., argue an interpretation), the context for the performance (e.g., in writing, in discussion), and the expected level of performance (e.g., scoring fifteen out of twenty on an established rubric). As Wiggins and McTigue (2005) have argued, it is hard to separate the learning goal from an *assessment*, because the expression of a learning outcome will necessarily identify a learner's performance within a specific context: e.g., write an essay, represent and evaluate alternative views in discussion, summarize in discussion and writing the plot of a narrative. So, in finding the language to note what students will be able to do as a result of their learning, look ahead to the assessment you plan to use to be able to see evidence of learning.

As noted throughout this book, in thinking about the *sequence* of inquiry and learning, begin with the relatively simple and move toward greater and greater levels of complexity. The introductory or "gateway" activity for the unit should activate students' prior learning and provide a point of entry into the exploration of a rich concept or complex problem. For a unit that focused on the concept of *justice*, a team of teachers introduced the unit with Chris Ware's provocative drawing entitled "Stop," which appeared on the March 14, 2016, cover of *The New Yorker* magazine (see McCann & Knapp, 2021). Another team of teachers began a unit about "Monsters in Our Literature, Monsters in Our Lives" with a reading of Maurice Sendak's *Where the Wild Things Are*. In either case, the learners already knew a great deal about the concept but grappled collaboratively to find the precise language and examples to define the abstractions of *justice* and *monsters*.

The richness of the central concept will invite a number of questions, and the questions will invite consideration of how authors have represented the problems and suggested answers or other complications. See figure 9.1 below for an overview of the unit architecture.

Concept

- ✓ Identify the unifying concepts, recurring themes, or "big questions" that connect a body of content that are important for the discipline.
- ✓ Identify the specific goals, standards, and target outcomes for a unit of study.

Rationale

- ✓ Express the rationale for studying the overarching concept: its appropriateness for a selected group of students, its complexity and interesting facets

Design

Design and sequence the appropriate learning activities that scaffold, align, and lead to the target outcomes.
Select and sequence the appropriate materials that will support inquiry into the overarching concept.
Provide for the appropriate assessments to monitor and support learning and to measure growth over time.

Figure 9.1 Big Picture of Unit Design. Source: *Author created.*

CONSTRUCTING COHERENT CONCEPTUAL UNITS OF INSTRUCTION

Step 1: **Select the *Concept* to Be Studied in the Unit**

- Learn all you can about the learners in your class: What are their proficiencies and their areas for growth? What are their interests? What are the issues in their lives and also in the lives of the members of their family and their community?
- Drawing from knowledge about the specific learners, the goals for the school and the district, and an understanding of the demands of the discipline, select a central concept that will unify study and engage learners in shared inquiry.

Step 2: **Develop the *Rationale* of the Unit**

- Explain why the central concept is worth studying for extended period of time.
- Justify that the inquiry into this concept is appropriate for the particular grade, developmental level, and interests of your students.
- Represent the many facets and richness of this concept in a way that makes it evident that the study of the concept warrants attention over multiple weeks.

Step 3: **Determine the Unit's *Learning Targets***

- In the end, what outcomes do you expect to see? In other words, how will the learners change as a result of their experience with this unit?
- If there are State goals and numerous standards related to what you are trying to accomplish, which standards are the priorities? How can you represent the standards in terms that the students can understand?

Step 4: **Develop the *Essential Questions***

- *Concepts* or *themes* are not the same as *topics*. There is a big difference between the generic topic of *identity* and an inquiry into why it is important to have a strong sense of identity.
- How can you cast a theme or concept in the form of a *significant problem* that will drive the inquiry during the unit?
- How can you represent the *overarching concept* as a *question* or *problem* worthy of a class's investigation?

Step 5: **Select and Sequence *Materials***

- Develop the introductory of "gateway" activities that link to prior units and/or prior learning and reveal consequential problems.

- Develop the preliminary lessons that build on the unit's concepts: Driven by the key questions, use materials and students' experiences to develop the concepts.
- Build lessons that allow learners to synthesize and test the central concepts.
- Sequence both materials and the activities that allow students to practice with generative procedures for reading, writing, and critical thinking.

Step 6: Design Lessons with *Activities* and *Assessments*

- Design learning activities that invite students to be actively involved.
- Invite students to construct knowledge.
- Rely on activities that promote collaboration and interaction.
- Build-in informal, formative assessments to track students' progress and to provide feedback that helps learners to set learning goals to make their own adjustments.
- Recognize the uniqueness of each learner and differentiate to address the variety of learners' needs.

Step 7: Provide for the *Summative Assessment* of Students

- Design the form of the assessment to allow you to make inferences about the students' learning of complex *procedures* and concepts.
- Design assessment procedures that require the *independent application* of the learned procedures.

SEQUENCING OF LEARNING ACTIVITIES

Again, three general rules should guide the sequence of learning activities. First, meet students where they are. If you are going to build instruction on the knowledge that students already have, you need to know about the learners and then tap into their prior knowledge and interests. It is always a good idea to learn as much as you can about students, but you can rely on the assumptions that adolescents have already thought a great deal about identity, maturity, freedom, authority, fairness, justice, privacy, friendship, and romantic love, to name a few possibilities. A teacher can easily find problem situations in the news or from pop culture that can prompt discussion and initiate inquiry.

The second principle is to begin with a text or activity that is relatively simple and then move forward to increasingly complicated problems and complex texts. The outline below (table 9.2) offers one example of a sequence of texts, problems, and activities. This would not be a loosely connected collection of readings, but a carefully orchestrated inquiry into the complexities of the texts and the themes they invite readers to evaluate.

The third principle is to move from activities that are highly dependent on the teacher's facilitation to more independent performances that draw

Table 9.2 Sample Sequence to a Literature-based Unit into *Justice*

Essential Questions	Text	Activity	Assessments
What is *justice*? What are the requirements of due process as a protection for justice? What obligations do witness to injustice have?	Jason Reynolds. *All American Boys*	Discussions of interpretation of an image that suggests a thematically connected narrative (e.g., Chris Ware's "Stop") Responses and discussion of justice opinionnaire Discussion of scenarios or news stories that depict situations in which justice might be questioned	Monitoring of small group and whole class discussions Exit slips that reveal questions and problems with the text. Written responses to the reading
What are appropriate responses to perceived injustices and to recognized offenses? When, if ever, is it appropriate to sacrifice the welfare of one individual to secure benefits for all other members of a community?	Kate Chopin. "The Story of an Hour" Guy de Maupassant. "The Necklace" Shirley Jackson. "The Lottery" Ursula Le Guin. "The Ones Who Walk Away from Omelas"	Read aloud/ think aloud demonstrations to illustrate interpretive procedures Through small group deliberations and whole class discussions, examine texts through various critical lenses	Monitoring discussions to see procedures in play Quick written responses to text Extended written analysis of a selected text
What are the appropriate consequences for those who seriously harm us or the people we care deeply about?	Edgar Allen Poe. "The Cask of Amontillado" Hernando Téllez. "Lather and Nothing Else" Ring Lardner. "Haircut"	Whole class and small group discussions of images and constructed passages to identify text elements that reveal irony	Monitoring of responses during discussions Quick written responses to texts

(Continued)

Table 9.2 Sample Sequence to a Literature-based Unit into *Justice* (*Continued*)

Essential Questions	Text	Activity	Assessments
When, if ever, is revenge an appropriate response to harms? How can we distinguish revenge from justice?		Enactment of a scene from a story or stories. Discussion of the thematic implications, especially the authors' possible responses to the class's essential questions	
Is it better to be merciful than vengeful? When, if ever, is someone or some group justified in subjugating some other person or some other group? When injustices have occurred, how is it possible to restore justice and achieve a sense of harmony?	Shakespeare's *The Tempest*	Read aloud/ think aloud demonstrations Enacting selected scenes of the play In small group and whole class discussions, examining the play through various critical lenses Viewing and discussing a live of recorded interpretation of the play	Monitoring the discussions Exit slips to reveal students' questions and understandings Elaborated essay analysis of the play, especially with references to the concept of justice and to other texts from the unit

from collaborative work but offer independent practice with the procedures for reading literary texts and writing about them. All learning is essentially social; but if learning is to be generative, students need to be able to demonstrate that they can apply procedures independently to new situations.

DEVELOPING LEARNING EXPERIENCES

Several texts will support teachers in finding the kind of learning activities that will help adolescents to read complex texts closely and critically. We list a few titles below. In addition to offering sample activities, these texts guide teachers in constructing their own activities to help students to become aware of procedures for reading literary texts.

Experience suggests that inquiry-based learning activities should have a few key features. As a means for reflecting on the possible efficacy and the likely appeal of any learning activity, teachers might review this brief list before teaching. After a lesson, teachers might return to this list as a way to reflect on why a learning activity or sequence did not seem to have the anticipated impact. Here are the key features:

- The learning activity should introduce a problem that learners find consequential.
- The problem that prompts the inquiry should help students to tap into prior knowledge.
- The activity requires student interaction: in pairs, in small groups, and as a whole class.
- The classroom discourse immerses students in the procedures that are part of the interpretation and evaluation of literature.
- The learning activity aligns closely with the stated learning targets and the assessments.
- Assessments are built into the activities, as a means for the teacher to monitor learners' performance and for the teacher to provide feedback to help students to adjust the practice.
- Assessments are a natural product of the activity: for example, the written response that the discussions prepared students to produce.

ASSESSMENT OF THE IMPACT ON LEARNING

As noted above, the means that a teacher uses to judge the impact that a unit of instruction has had on students' learning is in itself an expression of the learning targets for the unit. For example, a teacher might think that an appropriate summative assessment might be that *students will write an elaborated essay in which they frame a problem, express a position or response to the problem, represent and evaluate several perspectives, and advance an argument by citing and interpreting features of the text*. The prompt that directs students in what they should do also expresses a goal: for example, the specific performance that students should be able to accomplish as a result of their learning. A strategic teacher will look at this expectation and ponder what students need to know and need to be able to do in order to accomplish the performance successfully.

Of course, the prompt/goal expressed above embeds several objectives: that students can contend with an area of doubt, that students can attend to the interpretations expressed by their peers and perhaps by authors, that students can argue logically, that students can engage with each other civilly, especially when there are strong disagreements. If teachers have any regard for their students' development, they will be fostering these behaviors and looking for these behaviors throughout the unit. Teachers will also want to provide students with the appropriate feedback and coaching to allow the learners to make adjustments before any summative assessment.

In assessing students' performance throughout a unit of study, a teacher is also checking that the learning activities are having their intended impact. In this sense, teachers are assessing themselves: To what extent did the designed learning activities change students in some way? And can teachers help students to become aware of their own progress or their own performance against a given standard? If teachers can provide students with ways to reflect on their growth or their current performance against a recognized standard, students can set their own goals for improvement and become aware of what they need to do to improve.

If teachers are going to report to students and parents about students' growth as critical readers of literature, they need to have some basis for demonstrating that growth. In a conventional way, a teacher will have a baseline measure (e.g., a writing sample) at the beginning of the unit and a comparable measure at the end. For any discussion of growth to make any sense, teachers will need to check that a baseline measure like a writing sample is indeed comparable to another writing sample at the end of the unit. It means that for a literature unit, teachers should ask students to write an essay about a work of literature at the beginning of the sequence of learning activities and again at the end of the unit, with almost identical prompts. Perhaps the best that teachers can do is to check for "face validity," that is, the tasks appear to be appropriate ways to discover if students have read a text critically and that the tasks are about the same.

Another way of thinking about the impact of instruction is to measure students' performance against a reliable standard. If students could discuss a set of written responses to literature and decide that the responses have in common and describe how one essay might be better than the others, the learners can contribute to the construction of a rubric that sets a target for performance. When students are well aware of the standard, they can understand a teacher's feedback about the students' strengths and areas for growth in regard to the established rubric.

Writing about literature seems to be a natural means for responding to what one has read and seems a logical way to assess learners' understanding and command of interpretive procedures. It seems rather strange to have genuine discussions, performances, quick written responses, collaborations, and demonstrations throughout a unit and then test students through a forced choice test that emphasizes recall of discrete bits of information. In contrast, extended written responses align closely with stated learning outcomes and seem a more "authentic" assessment of students' learning.

RESOURCES FOR LEARNING ACTIVITIES FOR LITERATURE STUDY

Appleman, D. (2015). *Critical encounters in secondary English.* New York, NY: Teachers College Press.

Beers, K. (2003). *When kids can't read; What teachers can do: A guide for teachers 6-12.* Portsmouth, NH: Heinemann.

Johannessen, L. R., Kahn, E., & Walter, C. C. (2009). *Writing about literature*, 2nd edition, revised and updated. Urbana, IL: NCTE.

McCann, T.M. & Knapp, J.V. (2021). *Learning to enjoy literature: How teachers can model and motivate.* Lanham, MD: Rowman & Littlefield.

McCann, T.M. & Knapp, J.V. (2019). *Teaching on solid ground: Knowledge foundations for the teacher of English.* New York, NY: Guilford Press.

McCann, T.M. & Flanagan, J.M. (2002). A "Tempest" project: Shakespeare and critical conflicts. *English Journal, 92*(1) (September), 29–35.

Smith, M.W. (1991). *Understanding unreliable narrators.* Urbana, IL: NCTE.

Smith, M.W., Appleman, D., & Wilhelm, J.D. (2014). *Uncommon core: Where the authors of the standards go wrong about instruction-and how you can get it right.* Thousand Oaks, CA: Corwin.

Smith, M.W., & Wilhelm, J.D. (2010). *Fresh takes on teaching literary elements.* Urbana, IL: NCTE.

YOUR VIEW

This chapter imagines that a teacher would put into practice the instructional procedures recommended throughout the book, but practice within a coherent unit of instruction. The unit planning requires looking far ahead, perhaps across nine or eighteen weeks, and connecting the various texts, discussions, and other learning activities in one extended line of inquiry. Such a unit would involve students in problem-solving and critical-thinking every day, and the inquiry would build in such a way that the learning each day builds on the day before, and the discussions held each day depend on the preceding discussions. Such scaffolding is essential to learning and is satisfying to learners because classroom experiences emphasize the learners' competence and help them to feel connected to their peers. Perhaps you and your colleagues have other notions about how a literature-based unit of study should form. You might want to discuss the following questions with some other teachers.

1. How important is it that students can experience their study of literature as a unified and coherent whole?
2. If the study of literature does not have to be conceptually or thematically connected, what are the alternatives and why might the alternatives be better?
3. How do you typically plan for literature instruction? Do you operate chronologically? Do you emphasize a set of discrete skills? While you work on skills, how do you connect the learning across days and weeks of instruction?
4. What promise do you see in an inquiry-based approach to literature instruction?

Appendix
"Poor Alfred, Buried Three Times"
Nora O'Flynn

On the beach at the east end of Clare Island, County Mayo, Ireland, a body washed ashore. Children at play discovered the body, blue in the exposed flesh, entangled by seaweed, repeatedly washed by the rhythmic surf. The children screamed and ran to find adults to remove the corpse from the place of their accustomed play.

The year was 1925. The English still dominated the Irish and held most civil service posts, including those on Clare Island. There were two college-educated residents on the island—Father McNamara, pastor of the Church of the Sacred Heart, and Mr. McGreal, headmaster at Saint Patrick National School. Once every month, Father McNamara was allowed to leave the island and visit the mainland of Ireland. In his absence, Mr. McGreal was consulted for advice and enlisted for quasi-ecclesiastical duties. Such was the case on this August morning.

Tim O'Malley, a fisherman, and Pat Burns, a farmer, having covered the corpse and loaded it on Pat's cart, went to the home of Mr. McGreal to seek advice about the disposal of the body. The three consulted in the front yard of the McGreal home and decided without question that the body must be buried immediately. No one could properly identify the disfigured body of the man who had died. There seemed no sign of foul play, and death by drowning was common in the frigid waters of Clew Bay. Since there was no morgue on the island and no means of refrigeration to preserve the body, the three men recognized a keen sense of decency and a need for proper sanitation that the body must be interred as soon as possible.

Mr. McGreal collected his prayer book and a spade and headed to the churchyard adjacent to the ruins of a Cistercian abbey. Tim O'Malley ran to Cleary's Pub near the quay to recruit mourners for this impromptu funeral. On the way, he called to farmers in their fields to urge them to bring a shovel and meet at the churchyard. After all assembled and the grave was dug, the corpse of the drowned man, wrapped in a tarp from Tim O'Malley's boat, was lowered into the grave. Mr. McGreal opened his prayer book and said an appropriate prayer for the dead. The few in attendance lowered their heads solemnly and mumbled a Hail Mary.

By the time Father McNamara returned to the island the next day, word of the drowned man had reached many residents on the island, and it was discovered that the man was likely Alfred Kitchums, the lighthouse keeper who had gone missing for several days. Men at Cleary's Pub discussed the matter soberly until Fergus Gavan noted that Alfred, a government-employed lighthouse keeper, was Anglo-Irish and most certainly a Protestant. And, noted Fergus, shaking his head gravely, was this not a sacrilege for Mr. McGreal and his accomplices to bury Alfred Kitchums, a known Protestant, in the consecrated ground of a Roman Catholic cemetery? The men wisely concluded that something must be done to correct this desecration as soon as possible.

At a decent hour the next morning, the men from Cleary's Pub called on Father McNamara, who had returned to the island, to share their conclusions and to recommend action to exhume the offending body from the consecrated ground. Father McNamara judged it most appropriate to call on Mr. McGreal to hear his side of the story. Mr. McGreal invited the small party into his home for tea, over which they agreed that the unacceptable deposit of Alfred in the Catholic cemetery was a more honest mistake than conscious sacrilege, but they still needed to know what to do to correct matters.

Fergus Gavan offered that there might be some profit in consulting with Tim O'Malley and Pat Burns, whom he suspected was standing at the bar in Cleary's Pub by now. So the men removed to the pub, where they found Tim and Pat standing at the bar, leaning over their pints. After a quick review of the facts and the shaking of heads all around, the men were at a loss for a solution. There was only one cemetery on the island, and decency and safety called for the body to remain buried, yet sacrilege threatened the spiritual welfare and compromised the moral standing of all involved. After a bit of whisky and a second pint, Pat Burns offered generously to allow Alfred to be buried at the back of his potato field. He recalled that there was a small plot of ground that he allowed to go fallow each year, and he would have no difficulty with a Protestant taking up eternal residence near his potato crop. All the men saw the wisdom and generosity in this offer.

So, the next morning, the assembled men dug up the remains of Alfred from the churchyard near the abbey and solemnly carted him to the back of Pat Burns' potato field. There, before the prepared grave, Father McNamara said prayers for the dead and reminded all the men that death could visit them at any time, just as it had unexpectedly visited Alfred, and that they must be prepared to face judgment at any moment of their lives. They all recited a Hail Mary and crossed themselves.

The following spring, after the word of Alfred's death had reached many of Alfred's relatives and friends on the mainland of Ireland and in England, they began to appear on Clare Island, sometimes unloading from the ferry in small groups. The friendly residents pointed the way to Pat Burns' farm and described where to find the gravesite. It did not take many such visits for Pat to discover that the relatives and friends cut across his field, trampling the spreading potato rills and threatening his crop. Initially, he had been happy to accommodate the unfortunate Alfred, but he could not allow his crop to be ruined by these many visitors. Pat invited Father McNamara, Mister McGreal, and all interested parties on the island to meet at Cleary's Pub to seek a solution to the current dilemma.

The problem seemed at first unsolvable. Alfred's partially decomposed body could not be shipped off to England or another part of Ireland, especially since no relative would claim the remains. Pat Burns could no longer countenance visitors trampling his potato crop. Father McNamara made it clear that burial in the Catholic churchyard was impossible. Burial at sea would surely be disrespectful to the family. The men consumed stout and drank their whiskey. No one offered burial alternatives. When it neared closing time, old Paddy Cleary recalled the day when the Bishop came from Galway City to consecrate the churchyard. He remembered at that moment, with absolute clarity, that when the Bishop waved the aspergillum to sprinkle holy water across the cemetery grounds, there was a corner at the far right and closest to the abbey ruins where the holy water did not reach. The men perked up, looking away from their pints and directly at Father McNamara for confirmation. The obvious solution was that, technically, one part of the churchyard was not consecrated, and it would be acceptable to bury poor Alfred in this not quite holy plot of soil.

The next day was rainy and inconvenient for finding a group of men to exhume the body from the potato field. But in another day, the men assembled, and a few women and children, to move Alfred solemnly from a potato field to an unblessed corner of the churchyard before the ruins of the Cistercian abbey. Father McNamara prayed, men doffed their caps, and everyone looked solemn. Paddy Cleary stood erect.

References

Alter, A. & Harris, E.A. (2021). Dr. Seuss books are pulled, and a 'cancel culture' controversy erupts. *New York Times*. Retrieved from https://www.nytimes.com/2021/03/04/books/dr-seuss-books.html.

Applebee, A.N. (1996). *Curriculum as conversation: Transforming traditions of teaching and learning*. Chicago, IL: University of Chicago Press.

Appleman, D. (2014/2000). *Critical encounters in secondary English: Teaching literary theory to adolescents*, 3rd ed. New York, NY: Teachers College Press.

Ashton, H. (2018). "I'll come back and break your spell": Narrative freedom and genre in *The Haunting of Hill House*. *Style, 52*(3), 268–286.

Ball, D. (1983). *Forwards and backwards: A technical manual for reading plays*. Carbondale, IL: SIU Press.

Beers, K. (2003). *When kids can't read; What teachers can do: A guide for teachers 6-12*. Portsmouth, NH: Heinemann.

Bloom, H. (2001). *How to read and why*. New York: Scribners Touchstone Books.

Bloom, H. (1998). *Shakespeare: The invention of the human*. New York: Penguin/Riverhead Books.

Bouque, A. (2019). Planning, managing, and troubleshooting for rich discussions. In McCann, T.M., A. Bouque, D. Forde, E.A. Kahn, & C.C. Walter (Eds.), *Raise your voices: Inquiry, discussion, and literacy learning*. Lanham, MD: Rowman & Littlefield.

Boyd, B. (2009). *On the origin of stories: Evolution, cognition, and fiction*. Cambridge, MA: Harvard University Press.

Brooks, C., & Warren, R.P. (1943). *Understanding fiction*. New York: Appleton-Century-Crofts.

Carr, N. (2010). *The shallows: What the internet is doing to our brains*. New York: Norton.

Chappell, B. (2021). Dr. Seuss Enterprises will shelve 6 books, citing 'hurtful' portrayals. NPR.org. Retrieved from https://www.npr.org/2021/03/02/972777841/dr-seuss-enterprises-will-shelve-6-books-citing-hurtful-portrayals.

Coates, T. (2014). The case for reparations. *The Atlantic*. Retrieved: https://www.theatlantic.com/magazine/archive/2014/06/the-case-for-reparations/361631/.

Coleman, D. (2011). Discussion of the Common Core State Standards for English language arts & literacy and "Letter from Birmingham Jail" by Dr. Martin Luther King, Jr., Part 6. Albany: New York State Department of Education. Retrieved from http://usny.nysed.gov/rttt/docs/bringingthecommoncoretolife/part6transcript.

Collins, A., Brown, J.S., & Larkin, K.M. (1980). Inference in text understanding. In R.J. Spiro, B.C. Bruce, & W.F. Brewer (Eds.), *Theoretical issues in reading comprehension*. Hillsdale, NJ: Erlbaum.

Cuban, L. (1999). *How scholars trumped teachers: Change without reform in university curriculum, teaching, and research, 1890-1990*. New York: Teachers College Press.

Currie, G. (1997). The paradox of caring: Fiction and the philosophy of mind. In Hjort, M. & S. Laver (Eds.), *Emotion and the arts* (pp. 63–77). New York: Oxford University Press.

Csikszentmihalyi, M. & Larson, R. (1984). *Being adolescent: Conflict and growth in the teenage years*. New York: Basic Books.

Daniels, H. (2002). *Literature circles: Voice and choice in book clubs and reading groups, second edition*. Portland, ME: Stenhouse Publishers.

Davis, P. (2013). *Reading and the reader*. New York: Oxford University Press.

Dobson, M., Well, S., Sharpe, W., & Sullivan, E., Eds. (2016). *The Oxford companion to Shakespeare*, 2nd ed. New York, NY: Oxford University Press.

Ericsson, A. (2017). *Peak: Secrets from the new science of expertise*. New York, NY: Houghton Mifflin.

Evans, G., et al., Eds. (1974). "Hamlet," *Riverside Shakespeare* (pp. 1135–1157). Boston: Houghton Mifflin.

Fish, S. (1980). "What makes an interpretation acceptable?" *Is there a text in this class?* Cambridge, MA: Harvard University Press.

Fletcher, A. (2021). *Wonderworks: The 25 most powerful inventions in the history of literature*. New York: Simon and Schuster.

Forde, D. (2019). Seeing and hearing what actually happens. In T.M. McCann, A. Bouque, D. Forde, A.E. Kahn, & C.C. Walter (Eds.), *Raise your voices: Inquiry, discussion, and literacy learning*. Lanham, MD: Rowman & Littlefield.

Forde, D., Bouque, A., Kahn, E.A., McCann, T.M., & Walter, C.C., Eds. (2020). *Inquiry units for English language arts: Inspiring literacy learning, grades 6-12*. Lanham, MD: Rowman & Littlefield.

Gladwell, M. (2005). *Blink: The power of thinking without thinking*. New York, NY: Little, Brown and Company.

Goldman, A. (2006). *Simulating minds: The philosophy, psychology, and neuroscience of mindreading*. Oxford, UK: Oxford University Press.

Graff, G. (1992). *Beyond the culture wars: How teaching the conflicts can revitalize American education*. New York: W.W. Norton.

Graff, G. (2003). *Clueless in academe: How schooling obscures the life of the mind*. New Haven, CT: Yale UP.

Graff, G. (2008). How 'bout that Wordsworth! *MLA Newsletter, 40*(4), 3–4.
Graff, G. (2009). The unbearable pointlessness of literature writing assignments. *The Common Review, 8*(2), 6–12.
Graff, G., Birkenstein, C. & Durst, D. (2018). *They say, I say: The moves that matter in academic writing*, 4th ed. New York. Norton.
Grant, A. (2021). The science of reasoning with unreasonable people. *New York Times*, January 31. Retrieved from https://www.nytimes.com/2021/01/31/opinion/change-someones-mind.html.
Graves, B. & Frederiksen, C.H. (1991). Literary expertise in the description of fictional narrative. *Poetics, 20*, 1–26.
Greenblatt, S. (2004, 2016). *Will in the world: How Shakespeare became Shakespeare*. New York: Norton.
Hansberry, L. (1959, 2019). A raisin in the sun. In K.J. Mays (Ed.), *Norton introduction to literature* (pp. 1496–1570). New York: W.W. Norton.
Hillocks, G. (1999). *Ways of thinking; Ways of teaching*. New York: Teachers College Press.
Hillocks, G. (1980). Toward a hierarchy of skills in the comprehension of literature. *English Journal, 69*(3), 54–59.
Hillocks, G. & Ludlow, L. (1984). A taxonomy of skills in reading and interpreting fiction. *American Educational Research Journal, 21*(1), 7–24.
Hillocks, G., Jr., McCabe, B. & McCampbell, J. (1971). *The dynamics of English instruction, grades 7-12*. New York, NY: Random House.
Holt-Reynolds, D. (1999). Good readers, good teachers? Subject matter expertise as a challenge to learning to teach. *Harvard Educational Review, 69*(1), 29–50.
Homer, *The Odyssey* (1961/1998). Trans. Robert Fitzgerald. New York: Farrar, Straus and Giroux.
Johannessen, L., Kahn, E., & Walter, C.C. (1982). *Designing and sequencing prewriting activities*. Urbana, IL: NCTE.
Johannessen, L.R., Kahn, E., & Walter, C.C. (2009). *Writing about literature*, 2nd ed., revised and updated. Urbana, IL: NCTE.
Johnson, J.W. (1928). Dilemma of the Negro artist. *American Mercury* (December), 477–481.
Kade, J.F. (2020). An inquiry into what it means to be human. In D. Forde, A. Bouque, A.E. Kahn, T.M. McCann, & C.C. Walter (Eds.), *Inquiry units for English language arts: Inspiring literacy learning, grades 6-12*. Lanham, MD: Rowman & Littlefield.
Knapp, J.V. (2008). *Learning from scant beginnings: English professor expertise*. Newark, DE: University of Delaware Press.
Knapp, J.V. (2003). Family games and imbroglio in *Hamlet*. In J.V. Knapp & K. Womack (Eds.), *Reading the family dance: Family systems therapy and literary study* (pp. 194–218). Newark: University of Delaware Press.
Knapp, J.V. (2003). Introduction. In J.V. Knapp & K. Womack (Eds.), *Reading the family dance: Family systems therapy and literary study* (pp. 13–26). Newark: University of Delaware Press.

Knapp, J.V. (1984). Strategies for individual progress in reading literature and writing compositions. *The English Record*, XXXV, 1–7.

Krashen, S. (2011). *Free voluntary reading*. Santa Barbara, CA: Libraries Unlimited.

Lee, C.D. (2001). Is October Brown Chinese? A cultural modeling activity system for underachieving students. *American Educational Research Journal*, 38(1), 97–141.

Lee, C.D. (2007). *Culture, literacy, and learning: Taking bloom in the midst of the whirlwind*. New York: Teachers College Press.

Levine, S.R. (2013). Making interpretation visible with an affect-based strategy. (Unpublished doctoral dissertation). Northwestern University, Evanston, IL.

Mandler, J.M., & Johnson, N.S. (1977). Remembrance of things parsed: Story structure and recall. *Cognitive Psychology*, 9, 111–151.

Marshall, J.D. & Smith, J. (1997). Teaching as we were taught: The university's role in education of English teachers. *English Education* 29(4), 246–268.

Marshall, J.D., Smagorinsky, P. & Smith, M.W. (1995). *The language of interpretation: Patterns of discourse in discussions of literature*. Urbana, IL: NCTE.

Marzano, R.J. (2004). Building background knowledge for academic achievement. Alexandria, VA: ASCD.

McCann, T.M. (2014). *Transforming talk into text: Argument writing, inquiry, and discussion, grades 6-12*. New York, NY: Teachers College Press.

McCann, T.M. (2003). Imagine this: Using scenarios to promote authentic discussion. *English Journal*, 92(6), 31–39.

McCann, T.M. (1996). A pioneer simulation for writing and for the study of literature. *English Journal*, 85(3), 62–67.

McCann, T.M. & Knapp, J.V. (2021). *Learning to enjoy literature: How teachers can model and motivate*. Lanham, MD: Rowman and Littlefield.

McCann, T.M. & Knapp, J.V. (2019). *Teaching on solid ground: Knowledge foundations for the teacher of English*. New York, NY: Guilford Press.

McCann, T.M., Bouque, A., Forde, D., Kahn, A.E. & Walter, C.C., Eds. (2019). *Raise your voices: Inquiry, discussion, and literacy learning*. Lanham, MD: Rowman & Littlefield.

McCann, T.M. Kahn, E.A., & Walter, C.W. (2018). *Discussion pathways to literacy learning*. Urbana, IL: NCTE.

McCann, T.M., D'Angelo, R., Galas, N., & Greska, M. (2015). *Literacy and history in action: Immersive approaches to disciplinary thinking, grades 5-12*. New York, NY: Teachers College Press.

McCann, T.M., Johannessen, L.R., Kahn, E.A., & Flanagan, J.M. (2006). *Talking in class: Using discussion to enhance teaching and learning*. Urbana, IL: NCTE.

McCann, T.M. & Flanagan, J.M. (2002). A Tempest project: Shakespeare and critical conflicts. *English Journal*, 92(1), 29–35.

Miller, B.J. (2001). *Head-1st acting: A commonsense technique for young actors*. Hanover, NH: Smith and Krause Books.

Newstok, S. (2020). *How to think like Shakespeare: Lessons from a renaissance education*. Princeton, NJ: Princeton University Press.

Norris, B. (2010). *Clybourne Park*. London: Nick Hern Books.

Nystrand, M. (2017). *Twenty acres: Events that transform us.* Madison, WI: Wisconsin Center for Education Research. Retrieved from http://class.wceruw.org/documents/Twenty%20Acres.pdf.

Nystrand, M. (1997). *Opening dialogue: Understanding the dynamics of language and learning in the English classroom.* New York: Teachers College Press.

Nystrand, M. & Gamoran, A. (1991). Instructional discourse, student engagement, and literature achievement. *Research in the Teaching of English, 25*(3), 261–290.

O'Reilly, T., Wang, Z. & Sabatini, J. (2019). How much knowledge is too little? When a lack of knowledge becomes a barrier to comprehension. *Psychological Science, 30*(9), 1344–1351.

Palmer, A. (2004). *Fictional minds.* Lincoln: University of Nebraska Press.

Palmer, A. (2011). Social minds in fiction and criticism. *Style, 45*(2), 196–240.

Pearson, P.D. & Johnson, D.D. (1978). *Teaching reading comprehension.* New York, NY: Holt, Rinehart and Winston.

Phelan, J. (2005). *Living to tell about it: A rhetoric and ethics of character narration.* Ithaca, NY: Cornell University Press.

Pritiner, C. and Colaianni, L. (2001). *How to speak Shakespeare.* Santa Monica, CA: Santa Monica Press.

Prosser, E. (1971). *Hamlet and revenge,* 2nd ed. Palo Alto: Stanford University Press.

Rabinowitz, P. (1987). *Before reading: Narrative conventions and the politics of interpretation.* Columbus, OH: Ohio State University Press.

Rabinowitz, P., & C. Bancroft. (2014). Euclid at the core: Recentering literary education. *Style, 48*(1), 1–34.

Recht, D.R. & Leslie, L. (1988). Effect of prior knowledge on good and poor readers' memory of text. *Journal of Educational Psychology, 80*(1), 16–20.

Reisman, A. (2015). Entering the historical problem space. Whole-class text-based discussion in history class. *Teachers College Record, 117,* 1–44.

Rogers, C.R. (1961). *On becoming a person: A therapist's view of psychotherapy.* Boston, MA: Houghton Mifflin.

Rosenblatt, L. (1978). *The reader, the text, the poem.* Carbondale, IL: Southern Illinois University Press.

Rosenblatt, L. (1938/1976). *Literature as exploration.* New York: Barnes and Noble.

Rosenshine, B., Meister, C., & Chapman, S. (1996). Teaching students to generate questions: A review of intervention studies. *Review of Educational Research, 66*(2), 181–221.

Rogoff, B. (1990). *Apprenticeship in thinking: Cognitive development in social context.* Oxford University Press.

Smagorinsky, P. (2018). *Teaching English by design, second edition: How to create and carry out instructional units.* Portsmouth, NH: Heinemann.

Small, D. (2018). *Home after dark.* New York: Liveright.

Smith. H. (2015). *Teaching particulars: Literary conversations in grades 6-12.* Philadelphia, PA: Paul Dry Books.

Smith, M.W. (1991). *Understanding unreliable narrators.* Urbana, IL: NCTE.

Smith, M.W., Appleman, D., & Wilhelm, J.D. (2014). *Uncommon core: Where the authors of the standards go wrong about instruction-and how you can get it right.* Thousand Oaks, CA: Corwin.

Smith, M.W. & Wilhelm, J.D. (2010). *Fresh takes on teaching literary elements.* Urbana, IL: NCTE.

Smith, M.W. & Wilhelm, J.D. (2002). *Readin' don't fix no chevys.* Portsmouth, NH: Heinneman.

Spolin, V. (1999). *Improvisation for the theater*, 3rd ed. Evanston, IL: Northwestern University Press.

Spolin, V. (1986). *Theater games for the classroom.* Evanston, IL: Northwestern University Press.

Van Doren, M. (1953, 1939). *Shakespeare.* New York: Doubleday Anchor Books.

Vermeule, B. (2010). *Why do we care about literary characters?* Baltimore, MD: Johns Hopkins University Press.

Wellek, R. & Warren, A. (1949). *Theories of literature.* New Haven, CT: Yale University Press.

Weismann, G. (2016). *The writer in the well: On misreading and rewriting literature.* Columbus: Ohio State University.

Wiggins, G. & McTighe, J. (2005). *Understanding by design.* Alexandria, VA: ASCD.

Wilhelm, J.D. & Smith, M.W. (2014). *Reading unbound.* New York: Scholastic Press.

Wilhelm, J.D., Baker, T.N., & Dube, J. (2001). *Strategic reading: Guiding students to lifelong literacy, 6-12.* Portsmouth, NH: Heinemann.

Williams, J.M. (2004). *Problems into PROBLEMS: A rhetoric of motivation.* Fort Collins, CO: The WAC Clearinghouse. Retrieved from http://wac.colostate.edu/books/williams/williams.pdf.

Wineburg, S. (2018). *Why learn history (When it's already in your phone).* Chicago, IL: University of Chicago Press.

Index

abstract, 17
academic discourse learning, 62
accountability, 112–13
actions, 92, 95–96
All American Boys, 73
Allen, Woody, 112
Anderson, David T., 122
And to Think That I Saw It on Mulberry Street (Seuss), 62–68
Applebee, A. N., 75
Appleman, D., 61–62, 72
Aristotle, 5, 8
assign-and-assess model, xviii
The Awakening (Chopin), 16

background knowledge, building of, 12
Bacon, Francis, 5–6, 8
Ball, David, 95
The Bean Trees (Kingsolver), 19
Bellow, Saul, xv
Beloved, 73
Black Americans, 99–100
Bloom, Harold, 114
"The Blue Hotel," (Crane), 39
Bouque, Andrew, 75, 83
Boyd, Brian, 9

Campbell, Joseph, 44
cancel culture, 66

caricature, 67
"Charles" (Jackson), 68–71, 76–77
children, 65
Chopin, Kate, 16, 39, 77–81
"Chutes and Ladders," 92
classroom discussions, 76–87
classrooms, 7
close reading, xiii–xiv; of complex texts, 11–27; in university classes, xv
Clybourne Park, 107
Coherent Conceptual Units of Instruction, 122, 125–26
coherent literature curriculum, 118–19
Colombo series, 43
complex texts, frontloading encounters with, 11–27; background knowledge, building of, 12; complicated cases and, 21–27; group research project, 13–14; group responsibilities, 19–21; imagining experience, 17–21; individual rights, 19–21; matrimony, bonds of, 16–17; opinionnaires, 15–16; possibilities and cautions, 26–27; questions, 18–19; school scenario, 17–18; starting simply, 14–15; surveys, 15–16; teachers and, 11–27; thematic thinking, 15–16; transitioning to, 38–41
Crane, Stephen, 39

Index

critical views, 59–74; Appleman, D., 61–62, 72; complex text practice, 72–73; discussion, 72; Geisel, Theodor Seuss, 62–68; Jackson, Shirley, 68–71; *On Mulberry Street*, 62–65; on New Criticism, 62; reading Dr. Seuss text, objection to, 65–67; response to, 68; sequence to introduce/practice with, 62–63; short narrative, practice with, 68–71; Smith, M. W., 62; Wilhelm, J. D., 62
The Crucible, 73
curriculum, 117–32
Currie, Gregory, 5

Daniels, Harvey, 115
deduction, 5
delusions, 65
de Maupassant, Guy, 39
Dewey, John, 4
dialogic principles, 32–33
Dickens, Charles, 13–14
discussions, 32–35; authentic problems, framing of, 85–86; classroom, 76–83; knowledge domains and, 87–89; literature in, 75–89; from preparation to response, 86–87; written responses to literature, 83–85
distributed cognition, xvii
The Dynamics of English Instruction (Hillocks, McCabe, and McCampbell), 119

Eastwhist, N. S., 67
Emma (Austen), 26
Endeavor series, 43
exaggeration, 31, 35

The Fall of Sarah Maudlin, 48
fiction, 5
Fish, Stanley, xvii
Fitzgerald, Zelda, 12
Flanagan, J. M., 75
Fletcher, Angus, 5–6
Forde, Dawn, 75, 83

free choice reading, 110–13
free voluntary reading, 2–4
Free Voluntary Reading (Krashen), 111

Geisel, Theodor Seuss, 62–68
genres, 8–9
Gladwell, Malcolm, 21
Goldman, Alvin, 5
Graff, G., 61–62, 65–66
The Grapes of Wrath, 73
graphic image, 29
The Great Gatsby (Fitzgerald), 26, 73
The Group (McCarthy), 59–60

"Haircut," (Lardner), 39
Hamiltion, Edith, 119
Hamlet (Shakespeare), 73, 93–98
Hansberry, Lorraine, 98–107
The Hate U Give (Thomas), 73
The Haunting of Hill House (Jackson), 70
Henderson, the Rain King (Bellow), xv
Hillocks, G., Jr., 87, 119, 122
Hughes, Langston, 99
human beings, 9

I Am the Cheese (Cormier), 26
"impossible-to-study-for" evaluations, xv
incongruity, 31, 35
independent reading of literature, 110–16; free choice, with some accountability, 112–13; free choice reading, 110–12; limited reading choices from curated list, 113–15; literature circles/book clubs, 115–16
inductions, 6
Inquiry Units for English Language Arts (Forde et al.), 119
Inspector Morse, 43
instructional practices, 59–74
"The Interlopers," (Saki), 39
I-R-E (Initiation-Response-Evaluation) format, xiv
ironic text reading, 32, 34–35

Index

Jackson, Shirley, 68–71, 76–77
Johannessen, L. R., 75, 84
Johnson, R. Kikuo, 30, 33
journal writing, 14–15

Kade, Jane Feeney, 122
Kahn, E. A., 75, 84, 119
Kingsolver, Barbara, 19
knowledge: background, 12; declarative, 87; domains, 87–89; procedural, 87
Krashen, Stephen, 2, 4, 111–12

Lardner, Ring, 39
learning, 118–19
learning activities: assessment of, 129–31; experiences, 128–29; resources for, 131; sequence of, 126–28
learning outcomes, 123–24
Learning to Enjoy Literature (McCann and Knapp), xviii, 7
limited reading choices from curated list, 113–15
literary learning, 4–10, 32
literary pleasures, 3
Literature as Exploration (Rosenblatt), xvi
literature circles/book clubs, 115–16
Lord of the Flies, 73
"The Lottery" (Jackson), 68–71

McCabe, B., 119, 122
McCampbell, J., 119, 122
McCann, T. M., 75, 119
McCarthy, Mary, 59–60
McTighe, J., 123
memory, xv
The Merchant of Venice (Shakespeare), 119
Metaphysics (Aristotle), 5
Miller, Bruce J., 92, 96
Mulberry Street, critical views on, 62–65
"The Murders in the Rue Morgue," (Poe), 6
Mythology: Timeless Tales of Gods and Heroes (Hamiltion), 119

narratives, patterns for, 43–57
Native Son, Merchant of Venice (Wright), 19
"The Necklace," (de Maupassant), 39
New Criticism, xiii–xvii, 62
The New Yorker, 29–41
noticing/significance of text, rules for, 29–41; complex texts, transitioning to, 38–41; discussions, 32–35; instructional sequence, 29–32; ironic text, 32, 34–35; practice, 35–38
Nystrand, M., 81

O'Flynn, Nora, 50–56
Oh Brother, Where Art Thou?, 9
online discussion, 32–35

Palmer, Alan, xvii
Paradise Cinema, 45–48
Paradise Lost, xv
parents, 65
parodies, 35
patterns for narratives, 43–44
perceptions, 21
performance: actions, 92; *Hamlet,* 93–98; literature as, 91–107; preparing for, 93–96; *A Raisin in the Sun* (Hansberry), 98–107; Shakespeare's plays, 92; teachers and, 91–107
Persepolis (Satrapi), 122
Phelan, J., 92
Poe, Edger Allan, 6
"Poor Alfred, Buried Three Times," 50–56, 133–35
pre-reading activities, 12, 26–27, 65, 88
Pride and Prejudice (Austen), 26
progression, 92

quizzes, xiii

Rabinowitz, Peter, xv, 44–45
Radway, Janice A., 3
A Raisin in the Sun (Hansberry), 73, 98–107

The Reader, the Text, the Poem (Rosenblatt), xvi
reader-response (RR) methods of teaching, xvi–xvii
reading habit, fostering of, 109–16; free choice, with some accountability, 112–13; free choice reading, 110–12; independent reading of literature, 110–16; limited reading choices from curated list, 113–15; literature circles/book clubs, 115–16
reading literature, xiii, 1–10; complex inferences, 7–10; discipline of, 2–4; fostering, 109–16; "free" reading, 2–4; graphic image in, 29; learning to/from, 4–6; patterns/structures in, 7–10; pleasure in, 4–6; social connection in, 4–5; in supportive classroom, 8; teachers and, 1–10
Reading Unbound (Wilhelm and Smith), 4
reversal, 31, 35
The Road, 73
Rogers, Carl, 81
Rogoff, Barbara, 4
Romeo and Juliet, 73
Rosenblatt, Louise, xvi
Rowlings, J. K., 114
rule of attraction, 49
rule of journey and return, 49
rule of potential rise and decline, 49, 55
rule of resolution, 55
rule of reversal, 49, 55
rule of success, 49, 54
rules of configuration, 44–45; derived, 49; expression of, 46–48; further practice, 56; "Poor Alfred, Buried Three Times," 50–56; practice with, 49–50; recognition/awareness to, 48–49

Satrapi, Marjane, 122
scientists, 6
Segal, Mike, 36–38
Sendak, Maurice, 124
short narrative, 68–71
Smagorinsky, Peter, 119
Smith, Helanine, 7
Smith, Michael W., xvi–xvii, 3–4, 29, 62
"Snakes and Ladders of Abstraction," 92
"The Sneeches," 68
social minds. *See* distributed cognition
Social Minds (Palmer), xvii
Spolin, Viola, 96, 100
SSR. *See* sustained silent reading (SSR)
"The Story of an Hour," (Chopin), 16, 39–42, 77–81, 85–86
students' assessments, xiv–xvi
sustained silent reading (SSR), 111

table reading, 93–94
A Tale of Two Cities (Dickens), 13–14
teachers of literature, 4–5, 73; anticipation guides, use of, 15–16; in background knowledge building, 12; complex texts, frontloading encounters with, 11–27; on discussions, 32–35, 75–89; noticing/significance of text, rules for, 29–41; performance and, 91–107; rationale for, 122–23; and reading habit fostering, 109–16; reading literature and, 1–10; simulation/role-playing activity, 21–27
teaching, 7; complex texts, 11–27; literature/writing, 1–10
Teaching English by Design (Smagorinsky), 119
Teaching on Solid Ground: Knowledge Foundations for the Teaching of English (McCann and Knapp), 106
"Tech Support" (Johnson), 30–33
The Tempest (Wright), 19
textual analysis, xiv–xvi
Theater Games for the Classroom (Spolin), 100–101
theme, 84
tone, 84
The Tragedy of Cameron Lauterdale, 48

Vermeule, Blakey, 5
"Virtual Library of Conceptual Units" (Smagorinsky), 119

Walter, C. C., 75, 84, 119
Ware, Chris, 123
Weissman, Gary, 111–12
well-formed tasks, 8
Where the Wild Things Are (Sendak), 124
Whewell, William, 6

Why Do We Care about Literary Characters (Vermeule), 5
Wiggins, G., 123
Wilhelm, J. D., 3–4, 29, 62
Wineburg, Samual, xiv
Wonderworks (Fletcher), 5
Wright, Richard, 19
Writing about Literature (Johannessen, Kahn, and Walter), 84

Zombie New Criticism, 62

About the Authors

Thomas M. McCann is a professor of English at Northern Illinois University, where he contributes to the teacher licensure program. He taught English in high schools for twenty-five years, including seven years working in an alternative high school. His books include *Transforming Talk into Text* (2014) and *Literacy and History in Action* (2015). His coauthored books include *Raise Your Voices: Inquiry, Discussion, and Literacy Learning* (2019), *Discussion Pathways to Literacy Learning* (2018), *The Dynamics of Writing Instruction* (2010), and *Teaching Matters Most* (2012).

John V. Knapp is emeritus professor of English at Northern Illinois University, and, continuing since 2007, the editor of the literary journal, *Style*. Knapp has been an English teacher and professor since 1963, educating students at every level from middle school to doctoral seminars. Knapp is the author and/or editor of several other books, including *Striking at the Joints: Contemporary Psychology and Literary Criticism* (1995); *Learning from Scant Beginnings: English Professor Expertise* (2008), *Critical Insights: Family* (2013), and over fifty articles and reviews on literature, family systems psychology, literary criticism, and literature instruction.

www.ingramcontent.com/pod-product-compliance
Lightning Source LLC
Chambersburg PA
CBHW020125240426
43673CB00038B/597